The Way Forward:

The Church in this
Emergent Time

Brian,
Thank you for your
faithful witness and inspiration.
Your work continues to inspire
my work.
Jeff Kulling

Bestamar Publishing
5772 N. Camino Del Sol
Tucson, AZ 85718

Page Art by Mark C. Pedersen

Printed in the USA by Gail Watson Printing, Newberg, Oregon

Kallevig, Jeff D.
        The Way Forward: The Church In This Emergent Time
        non-fiction / by Jeff D. Kallevig
        ISBN 978-1-7321768-0-5
1. Religion

This book is dedicated to Karin,
the best partner on the trail I could ever imagine.

And to Ivan and Kasey, who make sure the path is never boring.

I Love You Very Much.

Table of Contents

INTRODUCTION

I am a Lutheran pastor, but this is not a Lutheran book. As a pastor I have served three congregations in very different settings. My first call was to an open-country church in rural Wisconsin, my second congregation was a suburban church in a suburb of Portland, Oregon and my third congregation is a church described as "a legacy congregation" right in the middle of Tucson, Arizona. This is where I am currently serving. All of the things I share in this book are experiences I have reflected on in my varied contexts of ministry. In the places I have lived, and done ministry, I have been richly blessed by the people I have served with, members of my congregations, and members of the communities around them. Civic leaders, teachers, business owners and many more, have taught me about God working in the world.

My wife and I have two mostly grown children and as a family we have always enjoyed outdoor activities: sports and school activities, but also backpacking, camping, hiking, surfing, travel and exploring. We have lived in places that offer boundless opportunities to be outside, and we have greatly enjoyed that.

It is important to point out that this is my starting point in sharing with you, the reader. These are the places I have been, it is where I come from, and you may come from a very different place. It may be obvious that the language I use comes from particular experience, like the church or the outdoors. I hope that when there are times my sharing sounds like jargon, you will still find meaning in it. I hope that if there are parts of my sharing you don't relate with, you will still find it relatable. And if there are times when my sharing sounds familiar, I may be talking about you.

This book is not an autobiography, or manual for ministry, or even linear. But I hope that it is useful in finding hope and meaning in community.

There are many authors right now who are writing and speaking truthfully about the changes we have seen, and are seeing, in the church. And the situation for Christianity seems to be growing ever more desperate. Spirituality and religious expression have changed drastically in recent years. Church institutions of every kind are experiencing decline. The world is changing rapidly. There is vast uncertainty about what of our Christian faith, expression, and institutions will survive the changes and challenges we are facing. There are a lot of desperate church people searching for hope and direction right now.

There are also many good and faithful authors like Phyllis Tickle, Diana Butler Bass and Brian McLaren, who are writing clearly and truthfully about the history of church and faith, and articulating the cultural shifts that have caused what is happening in our time. Things are changing, we can all feel that, but into what? We can see with varying clarity where we have been, but we can't see where we are going. That makes for challenging and uncertain times.

The Church in this Emergent Time

With all the assessment of where we have been, and how we got to where we are, there is still a foggy cloud bank that seems to be covering our vision of the church in the future. In this reality of uncertainty I hope to spread some hope, some focus, and some encouragement. It is my strong conviction that 'the way forward' is not as hard or scary as it may seem even when we are facing the difficult realities of aging membership, declining church attendance, and growing budgets matched with dwindling resources.

This will not be a manual for how to "right the ship" or how to bring young families back into the church. I am not convinced that either of those things will help, grow, or lead the church into the future. Instead I hope to show some examples of how we are the church, now today. As the Apostle Paul says "I can do all things through him who strengthens me." (Phil. 4:13) The "him" Paul refers to is Christ. And in Christ…

I am convinced that what the church is, is enough in itself.
I am certain that who we are can change people's lives.
I am confident that what we do is sustainable.

We will have to drastically change our perspective in order for any of this to be the case. The illustrations that follow are examples of the way we have been traveling, whether we realized it or not, and the continued way forward for the church.

As an institution the church is declining. Like every other institution in our culture there is suspicion and doubt. There is quiet desperation in every gathering of people of faith. They are desperate to hear news that is good, desperate to pass faith on to their children, desperate to see their grandchildren baptized, desperate for real relationships, desperate to save the institution that is the church, desperate for all kinds of things that seem out of reach. The desperation comes from the fear that the church they have known, loved, and feel responsible for may be coming to an end, and they feel powerless to save it. They may be right.

In the face of these kinds of uncertainty there is often a strong response that we should "get back to basics" or somehow re-create a better time by doing things the way we used to. Some may say we need to "get back that old-time religion." I am very convinced that will not work, mostly because it never has. Well-meaning people of faith have tried in every generation to reclaim some distorted view of what they thought was a better time. Not only is their vision of "how things used to be" an illusion, recreating the past has never been a faithful way into the future. But what I am suggesting may actually sound a lot like that. Bear with me. I hope we can find the way forward together.

In the summer of 2007 my son and I hiked with a couple of friends to the summit of Mt. St. Helens. After a peaceful night camping at the trailhead, we got up in the morning for the hike that would take most of the day. My son was 13 years old, we had been on many treks and camping trips together, and we were in good shape so we were prepared for the hike. It was a tremendous experience, and also educational. I grew up in the shadow of the mountain and remember vividly Sunday, May

18th, 1980 - "the day the mountain blew." But until this time, I had never hiked on Mt. St. Helens. Now, 27 years later, it was awe-inspiring to see how largely desolate the damaged landscape still was. That was especially obvious above the tree line. Most of the trail to the summit is in the rugged and barren terrain above the timberline. Once the trail comes up out of the woods and leaves the trees it really becomes less of a trail and more of a direction. It is hard to explain the vastness of the landscape in such a place, or how rugged it is. Above the woods, it is all boulders and scree field until you get within 100 yards of the crater's edge. And that last 100 yards is still loose, light, silty ash, even after 27 years. In reality it would be hard to get too lost because the great troughs that used to hold glaciers flank this path to the summit, and getting off course too far would require climbing equipment. So, for the first-time climber there is a lot of wandering back and forth to try to find "the trail" until you realize that the "path" to the top is not a trail, but a direction: up. To help hikers along the right direction there are markers: large piles of rock with a large pole sticking out the top. Each pile is roughly the same size, about six or seven feet tall, made of smaller rocks than most others around them, and the pole sticking out of each pile is about six inches in diameter and between five and eight feet tall. Very significant markers, called "cairns." Large and unmistakable . . . once you find it. But it is true that there were many times along the way when we stood next to one of these markers on the rugged, rocky terrain, and looked uphill to find the next one, and could not see it. So we would set off in an uphill sort of direction, scrambling over boulders and loose rock, until we caught sight of the next marker, and sometimes it was a journey of faith that there would be another marker. It was disconcerting, to say the least, when we would climb for quite a while and not see a marker. It was an obvious reality that the destination of our journey was uphill and home was downhill, but were we going the right way? Were we wandering? Could we get lost? Not having traveled this path before it was an unnerving part of the climb. And each time we spied a cairn we breathed a sigh of relief that we were headed the right way. This cycle of doubt and insecurity and then relief happened over and over that day. Even on the way back down there were times when we wondered if we had gotten off course, traveling for a long distance without seeing a marker.

The view from the edge of the crater was breathtaking and so worth the struggle to get there. In reflecting on the journey it was a journey that involved faith. Faith that the trail would lead the right way. Faith that the cairns were made by someone trustworthy (although the thought did occur to us along the way that someone could be playing a prank by moving the markers around). Faith that if we lost our way, together we had the skills to find our way home. And even more, faith that God was on the journey with us.

We never lost our way entirely that day, but there were many desperate, insecure moments on that trail. And the feeling of desperation sticks with a person. It hasn't tarnished the experience, but is a part of the joy and recollection of the climb. The cairns that mark a trail like that are reason to feel relief, and to give thanks for those who have come before us on the trail.

Christians have been on a faith journey since the time of the disciples. And in every period of history it seems there have been things we have disagreed about, and even fought over. But, there have also been some basic things that, believe it or not, we **haven't** fought over, like care for those in need. The command to care for the vulnerable (the widow, the orphan, the stranger) even comes from the Old Testament and has been direction for Jewish people long before Jesus. Jesus built on this tradition as a way of being in the world, and to follow his example is to be about caring for others, and especially those in need.

Over time the Church has fought over how to care for others, where to care for others, who gets to help, and how we decide who the "others" are that deserve our care. With those, and all the other things we Church people have fought over, there has been the underlying understanding that we should. We should care for others, and specifically those in need. Surprising as it might sound, here is something on which Christians have always agreed.

In all of its history the Christian Church has been on a path, somewhat the same path, of caring for others as a way of following Jesus. In times of division and controversy we have done it poorly because of the distraction of our own sinfulness, but we have still been following the same path. We sometimes use the language of our 'faith journey' or 'walk of faith' to describe following Jesus. For me this has always evoked an image of hiking. I am inviting you to ponder the image of us all hiking together. And even if you are a person who only camps at The Holiday Inn, you can still envision following a marked path. I invite you to consider the path you are following, to consider with new eyes what marks your path, and maybe even choose a new path to follow. Regardless of your religious conviction, practice or even denomination, there is something of our paths that we share. Some of what follows may bring up hard questions. I hope you have the courage to ask them. Some of what follows may be challenging. I hope you will engage in the opportunity to be challenged. Some of what follows may offer you information about the path, but may not offer clarity about where the path leads. I hope you will still find encouragement for the path we are on. While all of these things may cause us anxiety and make us want to retreat back down the trail we have come from, the only path we can take is the way forward.

So . . . let's go for a hike.

CHAPTER 1

Trail Markers

Since the beginning of time people have been making piles of rocks. "Cairn" is a Scottish Gaelic word that means 'man-made pile of rocks.' Every culture in all of history has had its reasons to pile up rocks. The ancient Israelites in the Bible were nomadic and would pile up rocks as an altar on which to offer sacrifices. Around the globe cultures have used stone piles to mark graves. Cairns have been used to mark property lines, places of importance, and have been used as durable monuments since the beginning of time. In some places and times they have been elaborately built and used for defense, or shelter. In many wild places in the world cairns are used as trail markers, and are essential for navigating difficult terrain where trails are not obvious. In the United States, from the sandstone and deserts of the southwest to the vast rock slabs above the tree line in the northern Rockies, as well as the trackless expanses of the prairie, cairns have been trail markers for centuries, even if they were called something else. For example, as pioneers were venturing west across the country in wagons it was common for people to get sick and die along the way. Their graves, very often marked by a pile of stones, became trail markers for those who would follow. There is a deep history, and even spiritual connection attached to these markers.

In a similar way, it is common to see a cairn alongside of a road today, in urban and remote places. Roadside shrines in many places mark a place where someone has died in a car accident. More recently these shrines have included crosses or flowers, but a pile of stones is often still a part of the monument. Roadside cairns also mark a place where someone has been. Whether something significant happened there, it is an act of creative expression, or a person just wanted to leave a mark, cairns are not accidental. Without written explanation it can be hard to know why a person created a cairn, but it is certain that they made it on purpose. In the Bible, in Genesis 28, Jacob has a dream. In his dream he sees a stairway that goes from earth to heaven, and God speaks a profound word to him. When he awakes he makes a cairn, although the language of the Bible says he "set up a pillar of rock" then poured oil over it and named the place "Bethel," which means 'house of God,' or 'place where God dwells.' Cairns are still used today to mark physical places of spiritual enlightenment. Coming across a random cairn while hiking in the woods always raises the question: what? What happened in this spot that was significant for someone? Was it a vision? A revelation? An epiphany?

In our faith journeys as Christ followers, often those places of divine experience are not solitary or remote. Very often the most profound experiences with God are connected with our experiences with others. On mission trips, retreats, or even in a Sunday worship experience, something holy breaks in on us and we experience God in a profound way. Those who have come before us have had similar experiences, of course. So, what if they marked those experiences in some way? Like with a cairn? It is my suggestion that the path we are on as people of faith is a trail that has markers, cairns if you will, that guide our way. These trail markers have nothing to do with doctrine, or denomination, or worship style, or any of the other things that Christians have disagreement about. Instead, this trail is marked by the basic ways we care for others. This trail has been a foundational and constant thing through our history, and even in times when we may not have been able to see where the trail was leading, we still followed, caring for others and hearing Jesus call us forward, farther down the trail. And each of these trail markers have stories that teach and inspire, a history that is far bigger than us. As we follow the trail markers we learn about following. We may not get any insight into where the trail is leading, and I'll admit, that can be disconcerting and scary. We are always comforted by the knowledge that those who came before us struggled and questioned the same things, and were just as disconcerted. But they modeled faithful following all the same, and even more, left markers for us to follow.

So let's get right to the heart of it. In the Gospel of Matthew, chapter 25, verses 34-40, Jesus tells a story about God. Sometimes when we read the Bible we read looking for our own stuff; what will this do for me, how can I use this, or how will this preach. Pastors are the worst. But let's try not to get distracted by our own baggage, and instead listen for what God might have to say. Let's not get distracted by 'blessing' and 'cursing,' or by 'kingdoms' and 'inheritance.' Instead focus on what God is looking for in us.

> *Then the king will say to those at his right hand, 'Come, you that are blessed by my Father, inherit the kingdom prepared for you from the foundation of the world; for I was hungry and you gave me food, I was thirsty and you gave me something to drink, I was a stranger and you welcomed me, I was naked and you gave me clothing, I was sick and you took care of me, I was in prison and you visited me.' Then the righteous will answer him, 'Lord, when was it that we saw you hungry and gave you food, or thirsty and gave you something to drink? And when was it that we saw you a stranger and welcomed you, or naked and gave you clothing? And when was it that we saw you sick or in prison and visited you?' And the king will answer them, 'Truly I tell you, just as you did it to one of the least of these who are members of my family, you did it to me.'*

The Church in this Emergent Time

There is an essential base in this story from Jesus that the church has used for centuries to understand, in simple terms, the trail markers that mark our path as followers of Jesus. But, as with most human endeavors or institutions, the church has always drifted away from the basics and complicated things with politics, doctrine, governance, bureaucracy and hierarchy. A significant part of the conversation among Christians with regard to "emergent church movements" is this question: If Jesus visited your church today would he recognize it as a group of people who are following him? Rather than dismiss the question in our defensiveness, or attack the questioner, just answer yes or no. Honest assessment of ourselves and our institutions is hard because we are vested and have taken ownership of, or at least comfort in, the strength implied by the institution. How can we get past that? Institutions are crumbling all around us, from political parties to the postal service. The reality of change in our culture and society is undeniable and can cause us to act out, retreat in fear, or redirect our anxiety in fighting over the furniture.

In all the times of fighting over popes and empires, over stained glass and stone, over doctrine and practice, over pipe organs and guitars, over carpet samples and fabric swatches, these things have always been understood as directions for our work and trail markers, or cairns, that people of faith have followed:

- Feeding the hungry,
- Quenching the thirsty,
- Welcoming the stranger,
- Clothing the naked,
- Caring for the sick,
- Ministering to the imprisoned.

What follows is contemplation and encouragement about what each of these looks like, and what they can mean for the church as we move forward. But I want the reader to understand there are two things that these trail markers are not.

First. These 'cairns' are not a new focus/program/ understanding/whatever that is going to save "the church" and bring back some storied time of success to your, or any other, church or ministry. The world, the church, and everything we have known about institutions is changing. There is no going back. These 'trail markers' are what we need to spend our time and energy doing as we move forward. Between where we are and where we are going, these are the things we do: not marking time, but making our time matter.

Second. These 'cairns' are not sequential. We can see, from scripture and our Christian tradition, that these are things we do in following Jesus. That is not to say we have to do all of them, do them in any particular order, or that we need to move from one to the other. Rather these give us focus points to direct our work. For example, you could ask the question in all the parts of your church's ministries; "How does **'this'** (*ministry, committee, program, thing-we-have-always-done, etc.*) lead our community in living out one of these 'trail markers'?" And I would even go further. If, when you ask that question, the answer is "it doesn't," then I would suggest you stop doing that ministry/committee/ program/thing-we-have-always-done/etc. because it leads you on the wrong path.

The really hard part of asking this question about our church or ministry is this: it means really changing what we do and how we do it. Here is an example. A piece of our collective conventional wisdom says that "a healthy congregation has a healthy Sunday

School program." But our collective understanding of a Sunday School program comes largely from a 1950's model of church. If you are one of the few churches that still has a Sunday School program at all, it may be hard to answer this question: "How does **Sunday School** feed the hungry, quench the thirsty, welcome the stranger, clothe the naked, care for the sick or minister to the imprisoned?" We may be able to come up with fine sounding answers about teaching faith to the young, and passing on the faith, but the truth in those statements is that, at best, we have taught young people what Jesus said, but not what disciples do. Unless the "Christian Education" program of a church includes, and is built around, hands-on living out of faith for the sake of the neighbor, its focus has been doctrine and dogma, not relationship and faith. The truth of this is borne out by this: how many Sunday School children from the last 50 years still participate in a faith community? I know it is harsh, but how long will we keep doing the same things, hoping to get different results?

If you are one of the many, many churches who have seen their Sunday School go away, I would venture a guess that there are those in your church who are grieving the loss. So the question is this: "How does **grieving the loss of your Sunday School** feed the hungry, quench the thirsty, welcome the stranger, clothe the naked, care for the sick or minister to the imprisoned?" I don't think anyone would say that it does. The majority of churches in my denomination have seen their Sunday School programs die, or they have tried to reinvent them, but even that struggles. What would happen if we changed our focus?

So often I have sat with dedicated well-meaning church leaders and the whole focus of our conversation is "how do we get youth and young families back in our church?" The question only really leads in one direction. No matter how you frame it, the point of the work is to build the institution of the church back to what it once was. This is really a sad use of time, emotion, energy and resources. The church of the past is going away. That doesn't mean the church is going away, it means that the church of the future is going to look different. And just because I don't know what that is doesn't make it less true. In this conversation there is one thing I know is true: there has never been a time in history when the faithful way forward was to re-create the past.

As we move forward in our journey of faith, both as individuals and as the church, it is hard to know where the path is leading us. But we can take comfort in knowing that we are not the first to follow this path, and we are not alone in following now. It might be helpful to think of the pioneers traveling west. We are like them. We will never forget where we are from, our tradition and history; it will forever shape who we are. That doesn't change our anxiety and uncertainty about where the trail is leading and what the church will look like when we get there.

The image of the 'cairn' is a useful metaphor to help us see that we are not the first to walk this ground, and we will not be the last. But tied up in our anxiety over the changes happening in our world, and the church specifically, are strong feelings of guilt and fear. We feel guilt over the notion that the institution our ancestors worked heroically to build and pass on to us is floundering or failing on our watch. And we are afraid of what the future might hold for an institution in which young people are less and less invested and involved. At the root of both emotions is the struggle with change and I would offer this word of comfort. In every generation the church has moved and evolved, some generations more slowly than others. And if our ancestors had been faced with the uncertainty and social shifting that we are, they would have found faithful ways to live into the future. So will we. As we look for the next generation of leaders to take the reins and guide the church into the future, they will come, but the institution will look different. The world is changing, so the church has to change. That doesn't mean God is different, or the message of scripture is no longer valid. It simply means, as it has in every generation, that the young will find their own experience and relationship with God. That will look different than it did for their grandparents or even their parents.

There is no single metaphor that answers every question, so let's not make more of this one than makes sense. But in this way of seeing our walk of faith, and the path of faith for the church, I am convinced there is wisdom that God has given in every generation. As we find our way forward may we be guided by the cairns left by those who have come before us, being careful to build them up as markers to guide those who come after us.

Here might be a good place for a word of caution. There are many historical ways people in every part of the world have used stones as markers and monuments. While they can both be called "cairns," I want to draw a distinction between a marker and a monument. Later (chapter 8) I will share with you a quotation from William Faulkner about monuments, but for now reflect with me about what monuments mean.

A monument is a way of commemorating something, or someone. From a statue in a park to a headstone on a grave, a monument primarily tells about the past. And even with the best interpretive plaque, it requires explanation and interpretation in order to have meaning in the present. But even with the best interpretation, the meaning lessens over time.

Many of the great cathedrals that adorn the countryside in Europe are exactly that, monuments losing their meaning over time.

Once on a trip to Europe I was blessed to stand in an efficient line to gain access to the Cathedral of Notre Dame, in Paris. While inside I was overwhelmed by the powerful history, artistry and deep devotion that went into building such a place, but also how it was meant to give glory to God. But I realize that my experience in that place has been largely informed by my life of faith lived out in Christian community. Not everyone has that experience, as I learned. While exploring the cathedral I was especially interested in the large paintings displayed in the niches along one side of the sanctuary, many of which date back to the 1600s. While I was leaning in to read the small print on an interpretive plaque, a family of four came up behind me to glance at the painting. Mom, Dad and two high school-aged kids paused briefly behind me. As they stopped the mother spoke to the family in a Midwest accent, loud enough to be heard by others but obviously unconcerned. She said, "This is disappointing. We stand in line to get in here and all there is is all this old religious junk!" Then they walked away toward the door. Dumbstruck, I could only gape. Later I realized what I wanted to say in that moment was, "This painting is older than your country, and has survived two World Wars! How about a little respect!" Instead I just stood there with my mouth hanging open, staring after them in disbelief.

The Church in this Emergent Time

In my reflection I realize that the Cathedral of Notre Dame is becoming, or has become already, a monument rather than a marker. The same can be said for cathedrals all around Europe. They are less markers that draw people deeper into an experience of faith, and more the monuments that commemorate the faith of those long dead. Is all of the western church going the same way, just at differing speeds?

As we contemplate the cairns that mark the trail for people of faith, may we be mindful of building up those things that mark the path for those who come after us, rather than building monuments that only point to the past.

For Further Reflection or Discussion

- What do you hope for the church?

- What do you think of the author's statement, "There has never been a time in history when the faithful way forward was to re-create the past"?

- Do you have experience following a trail? When & what kind?

- Is your church a monument or a marker? Why?

- What is your church most active doing, and how does that feed the hungry, quench the thirsty, welcome the stranger, clothe the naked, care for the sick or minister to the imprisoned?

Scripture for further consideration
Read Genesis 28:10-22.

This passage is often called "Jacob's Dream" or "Jacob's Ladder" because while sleeping in a desolate place Jacob has a vision of a ladder, or stairway, connecting earth with heaven. To mark the place where this vision happened Jacob sets up a "pillar of stone" (a cairn), pours oil over it as a sign of blessing and says "Surely the Lord is in this place and I did not know it!" (verse 6b) He called the place Bethel ("Dwelling place of God").

Prayer

Dear God, as we continue our journey of faith, trying hard to follow where you lead, may we let go of the fear of uncertainty and trust that you are the God who led our ancestors. Give us courage to look at who we are, and how we are, with honesty. We trust that you are leading us into YOUR future. In Jesus' Name, AMEN.

CHAPTER 2

Hungry

For I was hungry and you gave me food

Matt.25:35a

A Baloney Sandwich, with a Side of Grace

There once was a little girl. A little immigrant girl. She was eight years old and lived in a small town in South Dakota in the 1950's. She and her parents had fled from Lithuania during World War II. Her parents spoke very little English and stayed home on Sundays and read from a Bible they could understand while the little girl went to church. The little girl got a ride to church with the same family she rode to school with during the week.

One Sunday the pastor announced that there would be a potluck, and that members should bring food to share. The girl decided to attend the potluck and she went home and tried to explain to her parents about what a "potluck" is. The little girl's family was not poor, but had meager means. The following Sunday the little girl's mother made her a baloney sandwich and put it in small paper bag for her to bring and share. When she arrived at the church she went to the fellowship hall and near the kitchen was a long table with all of the dishes people had brought to share. There was the usual array of church supper hot-dishes, casseroles and goodies. Feeling very self-conscious and out of place, and realizing that what she had brought to share seemed inadequate, she quickly set her bag between the other dishes and slipped away feeling embarrassed.

As with all church suppers, nothing concerning the kitchen and the food goes unnoticed by the church ladies, and this occasion was no exception. A little later, as people were filing past the table and filling their plates, the little girl took her place in line. As she reached the place where she had left her bag she was a bit anxious, but the bag was gone and she saw that someone

14

had taken her sandwich, likely one of the ladies working in the kitchen. There, where she had left the bag, was a plate with bite-sized pieces of baloney sandwich, cut up and neatly arranged, with a toothpick in each. And . . . people were eating it.

This young girl's offering could have been rejected, disregarded, or ridiculed, but instead it was welcomed and used, and the grace of God was spoken to a young girl who thought she would be found lacking. She was not. With God, as with church suppers, no gift is insignificant, there is always abundance and there is always room for one more at the table.

That story is true. The little girl is an older woman now, and as she tells me the story she has never forgotten the grace and inclusion she felt in that experience. In our best moments we are like this. In the best parts of the church's history there are stories of welcome and embrace and grace. And there are just as many stories of exclusion and rejection. We know this, and we grieve our failures, but that doesn't take away the holy moments when we have lived up to our potential.

It is an interesting exercise to poll local churches and find out how many of them have 'food ministries.' Whether there is some sort of food pantry that distributes food, or a meal for the community, or food drives that gather food donations, it is extremely common for a church to have the instinct to feed people. It is also worth noting, that if you do a brief poll of churches in your area, you will likely find very similar efforts being carried out in close proximity. We have been great at "re-inventing the wheel," and we have also built great silos in which to house our ministries. We have been inspired to follow God's direction in our own way, rather than join with others and collaborate.

Here is a great example. The cairn, or trail marker, of feeding the hungry is in our DNA as people of faith. We know we are supposed to feed people, and when we do there is a holy experience, but then we take ownership of the 'holy thing' and make it something self-serving or separating. Instead of meaning in serving, we find meaning in leading.

Very often in places where there is a food ministry there will also be some conversation about "clients" or "populations" or "guests" or some way of talking about those who are being served. That dialog usually includes some concern about "double-dipping" or being taken advantage of in some way. It is well-meaning dialog but can easily slip in the direction of trying to figure out who is deserving, or it may slip in the direction of setting limits or boundaries so things are fair. Just a couple of steps in either of those directions gets us off the path of simply feeding the hungry.

There are many reasons for hunger in our world. But there are also many kinds of hunger. A few years ago my family and I were on vacation in Mexico, staying at a very nice resort. One of our days we spent several hours sitting poolside. A couple deck chairs away from us there were two teenage girls. Soon after we sat down and were starting to read and relax I noticed the girls engaging in their own small "photo shoot" on the edge of the pool. Taking "selfies" and posting pictures on social media has become common, and not just with teens. In this case it was hard not to notice as the girls took turns taking pictures of each other in provocative poses on the shallow edge of the pool. Then they returned to their seats and each tucked into their devices, I assume posting, sending, tweeting, whatever. I returned my attention to my book, and didn't think much of it . . . until it happened again. This time as one was striking an even more suggestive pose, the other stretched out prone on the pool deck, I imagine to get a more creative angle. Only this time, when she had taken the photos she remained lying on her stomach, blocking the path along the pool, for a longer time while she apparently posted and shared her photos. She was so lost in her own cyber world she didn't even look up when an older person actually tripped over her. When the two finally returned to their seats they sat for a bit, fully engrossed in their phones. And a few minutes later, they did it again, and again, and again. Over the course of three hours they took pictures of each other on the hammocks, on a bench overlooking the beach, in a half dozen poses and places, each time returning to their seats to spend 10-15 minutes "sharing" the experience, but hardly saying more than a few words to each other. They barely looked up from their phones when they were walking to any of these places, they barely spoke to each other while they were sitting next to us, and they were shockingly oblivious to anything happening around them.

There were older, probably retired, people around but there were also young people, specifically a couple groups of teenage boys. One pair of boys in their late teens, but clearly underage, had acquired a couple beers from their parents. It's Mexico, it's nearly spring break, some things go unnoticed, even stupid parenting. These two young men were nice looking kids and took notice of the two girls. For quite a while they took turns showing off trying to get the attention of the girls, at one point even falling into the pool right in front of where they were sitting. All to no avail, the girls did not notice. And when I say they did not notice, I mean they seemed to be unaware that there were any other people present at all. They were not being coy, or too cool; I was sitting close enough to hear them whisper to each other, but they didn't. Eventually the boys lost interest and moved on.

This is, of course, not the only place this sort of oblivious media-absorbed behavior happens. And it is becoming more and more a cultural norm. But what does it mean? About those two girl someone might say, "They were on vacation, having fun, doing what they wanted, and they weren't hurting anything." Or maybe one might make an argument that it was actually a good thing for them to stay in touch with friends on social media. The reality is that, for whatever reason, these two girls were unwilling or unable to engage with their immediate surroundings. The only thing that interested them about the sights around them were how those sights would look in the background of a selfie, or how those sights would be impressive to others online.

One might read this and see 'technophobe,' or curmudgeon railing about 'youth being wasted on the young', or some other complaint. But there is a snapshot of something important here. What is the hunger we are trying so desperately to nourish as a society? Because many of the things people hunger for are not food. Clearly smart phones, technology, and social media are not universal. But these things have become universally understood. When our laws need to protect us from texting while driving, and it is commonplace to see a person driving while talking on the phone, we have universally accepted some underlying things. We are not going to spend time here expounding on what all those things are. Instead ponder this, whether they needed attention, were massively insecure, or just vain, those two girls were hungry and chasing after something. It is in a community of faith where we can tell young people (and old people, for that matter) that you are enough, you are worthy of love, and even more than that, you are loved. Now ponder this: how are we (communities of faith) failing to tell people they are enough, they are worthy and they are loved? When we spend our time arguing over carpet and guitars, spending our money on crown molding and stained glass, rather than telling people they are loved by their creator, we are leaving them to satisfy their hunger in other ways. You know better than I the ways your community of faith struggles with this, as every community does, and it means we have lost the path and need to regain our bearings. When we get back on the path, focus on feeding people who are hungry, we can stop 'doing church' and get back to being the church.

Several years ago I read the book *Take This Bread* by Sara Miles. She shares her personal experience of conversion, and chronicles the creation of a food pantry at St. Gregory of Nyssa Episcopal Church in San Francisco. Inspired by her writing, and encouraged by her witness, I arranged to visit the food pantry and see this ministry first-hand. I made arrangements to stay in San Fransisco for a long weekend so that I could volunteer at the food pantry on Friday and join them in worship on Sunday, taking advantage of any opportunities in between.

The Way Forward

Friday there is an early prayer service in the morning before the work of distributing food begins, so I arrived early for my volunteering and was welcomed into worship. The church has a large, open, two-part worship space with lots of wood, artwork and ornamentation. Beautiful and intricate like many places of worship. During a brief time of fellowship, after the prayers, I said I was there to work as a volunteer for the day and was told that the 'foreman' would show up soon and we could get to work. Thinking there must be a fellowship hall or multi-use space for "the work" I asked where to go, and was told to stay right here . . . in the sanctuary. I milled around appreciating the artwork for only a few minutes, when the work began . . . in the sanctuary. Throw a cover over the altar in the middle of the room, move the candle stands to a side closet, bring out the rack with name tags for the volunteers and set it up on the altar next to some muffins and juice, then start rolling out tarps to cover the decorative hardwood floors. The sanctuary, the very center of worship for this community, transformed into a warehouse. The delivery of food arrived and volunteers worked hard bringing in pallets and bins of all sorts of staples, cans and dry goods, as well as mounds of fresh produce. Bins were stacked in orderly sections on the tarp, and in several places produce was poured out and piled right onto the tarps, which I was constantly mindful was a very thin veil between food and those beautiful floors. But, this is where the work happened . . . in the sanctuary.

It was a long day of hard work. I stayed and helped until the very end, wanting to experience every part of what they do. In the end I saw the sanctuary space transform back into a worship space that matches more of my expectations for a church. And I really felt a bit of shame at that realization. The work done in that space that day, around that altar, was no less an act of worship and no less of a holy thing. How full of ourselves we can be as church people.

The truth of that understanding was even more powerfully poignant as the community gathered for worship Sunday, processed around that altar and shared the Eucharist. The Lord's Supper, the holy meal at the heart of much of Christian worship, shared around the same table, in the same space as the feeding ministry days before. A holy meal, given and shed **FOR YOU!**

I worked for one long day as a volunteer, setting up, distributing food, and cleaning up after. It was an amazing experience in many ways, but a focused reflection for me was this. Although there might be many opportunities to become clique-ish or choosy about whom to help, they seem to have avoided those distractions. After meeting the variety of people they feed, I can see how easy it would be to become choosy. In her book Sara describes the temptation toward these struggles, but they seem to have kept the focus on the call to 'feed the hungry,' Friday or Sunday. They work within only the most basic of framework for an organization, and there seemed to be only two limits I could see. The first is an obvious limit to the food available, which varies widely week to week, and the second is that they try to ration how much of each thing a person or family can take of each kind of food in order to feed the most number of people. And even at that, each week there are those they can not help. There were many other things I learned about myself and ministry while working at that food pantry, but for now I would say Sara Miles' writing is a great encouragement in seeing the cairns marking our trail. *"For I was hungry and you gave me something to eat."*

What would our church be like if, like the food ministry at St. Gregory of Nyssa Episcopal Church in San Francisco, we used our holy space for the holy work of feeding the hungry with real food? Would our love for our hardwood floors outweigh our love for our neighbor? Look at your church budget, staff and facilities. How much of it benefits others? And how much is self preservation? In each of our communities, even the newest church, there has been a time when we gathered for food and fellowship, when even the least was welcomed, and even the least of our gifts was cherished. We can't go back to the way things were, but we can nourish those traits in our present ministry, and guard them for the future.

In my faith tradition as a Lutheran Christian we hold two liturgical rituals up as special, and call them sacraments: Baptism and Communion. And here is the best example of Christians fighting over who is worthy, rather than feeding the hungry. Lutherans hold that the two sacraments are set apart by these three things: Jesus told his followers to do this, there is a physical element, and there is the promise of forgiveness given with each. While it is true of other denominations as well, there are small branches of the Lutheran tradition that have focused largely on some specific rituals created by the church over time, but that are not necessarily from the Bible.

The practice of "closed Communion" usually has two basic understandings and requirements that make my point. First, those receiving communion must be approved by the pastor ahead of time to insure that they are penitent "true believers" (members of OUR denomination) and not unworthy imposters (members of any other Christian denomination). If being "rightly prepared" or holding the correct belief were the point, Jesus would have refused to give the bread and wine to Judas in the upper room - but he didn't. When Jesus says this is "for you" he meant even Judas. *(See Luke 22:14-23. And I know there are zealots out there who will accuse me of cherry-picking a text that makes my point, or ignoring St. Paul, so go look for yourselves. There is no exit of Judas from the upper room in Matt. 26:20-30, Mark 14:17-25, and even in John 13:26-30 Judas leaves after receiving the bread and wine Jesus gives him.)*

The second thing that seems to be a sticking point is the conviction that one must first be baptized in order to be welcome at the Lord's table and receive the bread and wine. Seems an odd distinction for us to make, since Jesus regularly ate and drank with "sinners." That was one of the Pharisees' main criticisms of him. Also, there is no evidence whatsoever that any of the disciples were baptized, yet Jesus began this new ritual with them. If Jesus includes those who are not qualified according to our "tradition," and offers forgiveness to those who don't deserve it, maybe we should re-think our ritual.

I have been blessed and humbled as a pastor to be the administrator of this sacrament week in and week out in the lives of the communities I have served. It is clear that each person who comes forward to receive the bread and the wine comes with their own understanding of this ritual and experience of Jesus.

It has always been my practice to look each person in the eye when I say, "the body of Christ, given for you," or "the blood of Christ, shed for you." And you might be surprised how hard that eye contact can be. It is an emotional and diverse experience. Some people return my gaze, some even hungrily and expectantly, and yet others keep their eyes downcast in humility and submission, refusing to look up. Some people are silent, but there are various spoken responses people choose as well: "Thanks be to God", "Hallelujah" or simply "Amen." There is a couple in my current context who have their own call and response to the sacrament; the husband says "He lives" when given the bread, and the wife responds "He lives indeed!" While it occasionally distracts me, I can get over it because I know it is an expression of faith, deep and heartfelt. And there are the silent gestures people use when receiving the sacrament, like genuflecting, that is making the sign of the cross on oneself as a reminder of being marked with the cross of Christ. I have even known a man who silently makes the sign of the cross over the bread or wafer, one hand over the other, before eating it. All are ways that we come to the table to be fed by the bread and wine, the body and blood of Jesus.

So even in worship each week, communities of faith speak of feeding the hungry. We have always known we should; nourishment is the most basic of human needs. And still we get distracted by deciding who is worthy. May we instead find the inspiration to feed the hungry, even as we hear Jesus say to us, "Take and eat, this is my body, given for you."

For Further Reflection or Discussion

- What are ways that your church gathers around food? Is that the same as feeding the hungry?

- What are different ways that people "hunger" in our world?

- What are ways that our worldly "hungers" are fed, but not nourished?

- What would happen at your church if you used the worship space for a food pantry each week? Could you? Why or why not?

- What is your experience, and practice, of communion?

Scripture for further consideration
Read Mark 6:30-44

There are six places in the Gospels where Jesus miraculously feeds a large crowd: Matthew 14:13-21, Matthew 15:32-39, Mark 6:30-44, Mark 8:1-10, Luke 9:10-17, John 6:1-14. In each of these places there is a great excess left over, even though the means were so meager in the beginning. How is this blessing and breaking of bread like communion?

Prayer

Dear God, even as you continue to feed us, nurture in us the desire to feed others. Lead us away from wrangling over who is worthy, and toward sharing your sustaining presence. And may providing for the basic needs of our neighbors become more important than preserving our buildings. In Jesus' Name, AMEN.

The Way Forward

CHAPTER 3

Thirsty

I was thirsty and you gave me something to drink

Matt. 25:35b

Sometimes it happens, through a series of insignificant circumstances you find yourself in tremendously significant position, or place, or conversation. That's how it happened. I recently found myself in one of those situations having breakfast with a retired couple who were very proud to tell me about the way they lived in retirement. They were "foot-loose and fancy-free." They traveled. They were very proud of their travels, and loved sharing their "stories from the road." They also loved to drive, and would travel by car most frequently. They had also decided a long time ago that renting a car for a trip was the best way to go. So they would rent a car for a trip to see friends, or for a weekend excursion, or just because. And when they went, they were never concerned with time. They would just travel where and when they wanted. On many occasions a short trip turned into an epic odyssey. They told me about recently renting a car for a three-day trip, and six weeks later deciding to head for home from where they found themselves on the other side of the country. Clearly they were gratified in having the means to do what they wanted, go where they wanted, and stay for as long as they liked. God bless them. They have obviously been successful in life, and are soaking in the experience of freedom as a result.

There was something else to this conversation though. In a conversation that lasted more than an hour this couple was very friendly, polite, and fun to talk to, but didn't really ask about anyone else. They wanted to talk about themselves, and tell others about them. They were polite, as I said, but it was clear that their listening to others was for the sole purpose of finding an opportunity to tell a story about themselves.

By the end of our time together I could see a quiet desperation below the surface. In all their stories of travel and experience, they were looking for something. When I met them over breakfast they were in the middle of a new odyssey. They had been on the road for a week and had no idea where they were going next. Clearly they had not found what they were looking for, and didn't seem too sure of where to look for it. In fact it didn't seem as if they were even aware they were searching. But when asked about certain things, like owning a vacation property, they bristled. Too much tying them down. When asked where they were going next, or where else they would like to travel, the only answer they would give was "where ever we feel like." As if making plans or setting goals was too much commitment. They reveled in wandering, and I can see some romantic beauty in that.

I could also see clearly that there was a desperation underlying their stories. A real hungering and thirsting for . . . what . . . for something. I'm sure they would have rejected the idea that they were looking for anything because they were just doing what they wanted. But there was certainly something driving them, something they were chasing after, something they were seeking but not finding. If nothing else, they were clearly looking for validation of their stories, evidence that others approved or were impressed. But again, they seemed unable to see that they were searching.

There are many, many people in our lives just like these folks, desperately thirsting for something they can't quite quench. Searching for meaning, or wholeness, or purpose, and looking with all the resources of an affluent culture, but still not finding it because it is not for sale. What they are thirsting for is *Authentic Community*. This is not something you find alone, or by focusing on your own path. Authentic community is built around three things; *honest relationships, shared passion in service* and *mutual accountability.*

Accountability is a hard word. Most people are defensive about the idea of being held accountable, as if being honest and vulnerable with others is somehow giving up the right of autonomy. But accountability is an essential part of any honest relationship. Being in community requires mutual accountability, not from a place of authority or rule enforcement, but from a place of care. True community is not coercive, but caring.

A group gathered around a *shared passion* can take many forms. For authentic community to grow in this passion, there needs to be some way the passion serves a greater good. Groups gather around shared enthusiasm for crafts, or card games, or social activities, but something deeper happens when a group gathers around service. There is something spiritual and emotional in the experience of a gathering that serves a greater purpose than ourselves, whatever form that takes. In the church we talk about caring for the vulnerable, feeding the hungry, and standing up to advocate for justice. But groups gathered around a shared passion for service can take many other forms. It is important to note that some significant things have changed in our most recent generations. Fewer and fewer groups are gathering around a shared passion for an institution, whether that be church, community, or political institutions. More and more groups gathering around shared passion won't necessarily be a part of an institution, and if they are it will be an institution that is seeking to build *authentic community.*

Foundational for authentic community is *honest relationships.* It may sound simplistic, or even naive, but it is basic. And it is hard because in a society with a high divorce rate and so many obvious signs of brokenness and dysfunction in our families, defining "honest relationships" gets really complicated. So let's just keep it simple. Honest relationships in authentic community start with socio-economic leveling. How's that for simple? Sounds complex, but what I mean is this: relationships are built on who people are, not what they earn, own or do. Or even more simply put, relationships are with people, not their possessions. That leads to the second step in nurturing honest relationships: mutual respect. Respect for each other, especially in relation to our differences, changes the dynamics of our relationships in infinitely positive ways. It is, of course, much harder in practice, but communities that seek to nurture honest relationships in these two ways are far more authentic.

Authentic community can also be more complicated, for sure. This list of three things is not meant to be total or definitive. We are all searching for *authentic community* that includes *honest relationships, shared passion in service* and *mutual accountability*. So many people today are searching for these three things, but don't know that is what they are looking for.

How do we reach those who don't even know they are searching? Maybe we can't. The best we can do is work to nurture authentic community in our own place, and work to be inclusive. My breakfast companions may never find what they are looking for, but hopefully in the time they spent with me they got a glimpse of something they could be a part of. They may never admit that they are thirsting for something more because that would require admitting that they lack something, and they were too proud.

People of faith have something life-giving to offer a thirsty world, and it is not our theology, our structure or our institution.

We have the capacity to model life-giving authentic community that nourishes our thirst for something greater, cares for others, and makes our world a better place.

In the congregation I serve there is a group of men who gather resources once a month and make a full-on sit-down dinner for a local men's shelter. They have been doing it a long time and they make the same things each month. They claim it's all they know how to cook, but it's good.

Each month the crew varies but the key leaders, and the menu, do not. Roasted chicken, mashed potatoes, tossed green salad, dinner rolls, and unfrosted bundt cake. They serve 100.

The process looks like this every month. A week ahead the word goes out to "the women of the church" that they need the bundt cakes. They need the same number each month, they want them unfrosted, and it is not purposeful but this is the only way "the women of the church" are asked to help. It just seems to be a guy's thing: men cooking for a men's shelter. A couple of days prior to the meal a leader shops for the food, buying mostly the same things from the same places, a lot from Costco.

The day of the meal they gather in the church kitchen early in the afternoon and start cooking. They spread the chicken out on large pans, season them, then bake one pan at a time. There are two ovens, one that cooks better than the other, so they rotate the pans as they cook them. Once a pan is done, they transfer the chicken to deeper serving pans and keep them covered and warm. It takes all afternoon. While that is happening there is a crew working on two big bags of potatoes: peeling them, washing them, cutting them up, boiling them, mashing and mixing them.

It takes all afternoon. The salad is easy. They buy salad mixed in a bag, the nice kind with berries and nuts, and mix it together in a bowl with dressing. The unfrosted bundt cake is cut into portions, stacked on a large jelly roll pan and covered. They cook all afternoon, then at dinner time (also rush hour) they load the food up, careful to keep it hot, and truck it across town to the shelter where they get help bringing the food into the cafeteria and then serve it.

The processes of gathering the food, preparing, cooking, etc. are all written out on several typed pages and kept in the "if I get hit by a bus" folder so if someone else needed to take over they would understand the oven rotation and the timing for cooking, the potatoes in the two biggest pots, and all other needed details. All the details but one: why?

Why? Why don't you buy already roasted chickens and cut them up? Why don't you get instant potatoes and doctor them up so they taste just as good? Why don't you find quicker ways to make the dinner? Why not find cheaper ways to make the dinner? Why bundt? Why?

All these and any similar questions receive the same blank stare as response. Simply put, the answer is "because." Because this is how we want to do it.

What the volunteers have found in this outreach is Authentic Community. The *shared passion* brings them together to serve others, they care for each other along the way in *honest relationships* and they have *mutual accountability*. It is a powerful witness, and ministry just like this is happening at churches in every town in every part of the country.

I know this chapter is called "Thirsty" and it may seem an odd example to share a story about a ministry that feeds the hungry. But this also nourishes a thirst. So often feeding the hungry, or any of the truly giving outreaches that churches engage, slakes our thirst for Authentic Community. Our "thirst" is satisfied by truly making a difference in the lives of others.

Here's the scene. My wife and I are at the Portland City Grill having a drink. We are sitting right next to the piano where an amazingly talented young man is playing. At the moment he is playing "Faithfully" by Journey, a classic 80's ballad, and some people are singing along. Beyond the piano is a row of pub tables full of people, and beyond that are the wrap-around windows with panoramic views of the city. It is bright and sunny, and the scene is light and festive. Something unusual catches my eye. At the table just beyond the piano there are two couples. Two men seated across from each other, one facing me and one facing away, and two women sitting on either side of the men, facing each other. One of the women has her feet tucked under her seat and is wearing stylish heels, and it is the heels of her feet that catch my eye. There is a very thin strap on the back of each shoe that is very low on each heel. It looks like the straps are just about to slip off, but they don't move. I think to myself, "it looks like those straps are desperately hanging on." It takes me a moment to recognize what is drawing my attention. This woman's feet are as still as stone, even with animated conversation going on at her table.

It drew my attention and as I spent the length of the song contemplating what I was seeing, I realized the straps of this woman's shoes were not the only desperate things. The woman was wearing a nice, stylish dress, but an older style. She was in her late 50's and cute. And although she seemed pleasantly engaged in the group conversation, her body language and posture were quite rigid and focused on her husband, who didn't seem to notice. He was the man seated facing me. He was wearing a bright polo shirt tucked into khaki shorts, both of which were starched and pressed, and loafers with no socks. He was a little older, early 60s, and clearly had a very formal attitude about his casual attire. His posture, like his wife's, was stiff. His attention was very intense, even rigid, and focused squarely on the man sitting across from him. His expression was pleasant, but seemed forced. He had sharp features, hair slicked back at a receding hairline, and had clearly deferred the seats with the better view to the other couple. There was something this man definitely wanted from the man facing away from me, and I could see more desperation quietly below the surface of what seemed like a forced casual engagement.

The other couple, by comparison, were far more relaxed in posture and countenance. The man's shirt was a floral print, nice but not tucked in or pressed like the first man's clothes. The second woman's attire was also more casual, nice but less formal than the first woman. And she was wearing loose flip-flops, in contrast to the first woman's stylish pumps, which remained tensely motionless. The second couple's posture was far more relaxed, I would even say slouchy. They were at ease and enjoying themselves.

It was obvious the man whose face I could see was desperate for something in this conversation. Maybe the man's business was failing and needed an investor. Maybe the man needed a connection with a younger, more powerful executive in his company because his job was at risk. Maybe the man was working to maintain a social connection to help his political position. It was summer and the atmosphere was casual like a weekend can be, but clearly there was something riding on this conversation. Was it business, or political, or social? I won't speculate further, although this restaurant is a place many wealthy and important people frequent. The observation is simply the desperation I could see just below the surface.

The woman's rigid posture and motionless feet first drew my attention, but the obvious desperation was what I saw in a deeper way. A quiet desperation for something. Maybe she was desperate to support her husband. Maybe she was desperate to be noticed by him. Maybe she was desperate to show that she was the kind of wife that could satisfy him, hold on to him, help him? Something. Whatever it was she was desperate for, her focus was on him, and represented in the stiffness of her posture, the tense stillness of her feet and the heel straps desperately hanging on.

Regardless of the accuracy of my observations, something large and true was reiterated for me in considering this scene. I may be off-base and none of what struck me might be true, but the truth in the observation is this: there are desperate people all around us, and it is easy to just gloss over the surface and not notice. There are desperate people in every business, in every office, in every institution. And we encounter them on street corners, while shopping, and even in our own homes. There are also many desperate people in the church today. The church is no refuge from the realities of our world. Like every other place in our world where there is struggle and fear, the church can seem to be full of desperate people.

The Church in this Emergent Time

People deal with fear differently, but it is very common for people to redirect fear and anxiety at an easy target: change.

A reality in many communities of faith is that families are setting different priorities than they used to. Bringing their children for faith education and indoctrination is less of a priority, or worse, seen as a bad thing. Children's activities and sports are given more priority than worship or faith formation. In my tradition Sunday School is the assumed norm for faith formation, but many churches don't have enough children participating to maintain a functioning program. So we struggle with the emotional reality of feeling like there is not a 'next generation' to take our place in running the church. In conversations about this there is often language about teaching young people the faith, or passing on the faith. In truth, the church has actually done a great job of teaching about what is important in this "faith" or that "church." It doesn't take a grownup to see that what a "faith community" spends most of its money on is its priority. And Christians of every denomination have succeeded in teaching that RIGHT belief or RIGHT practice is more important than RIGHT relationship. Doctrine, theology, and being right have become more important than knowing and being known. (Before you get your undies in a bunch I will point out that I said "Christians of every denomination" not "every Christian denomination." There is a difference.) Often the loudest voices representing Christians are those who stress being right over being loved, who focus on the letter of the law rather than the Spirit of love, who believe they can only be 'in' if others are 'out.' The church has done an excellent job of teaching this, society has decided that they disagree, and our "children and young families" have clearly said this with their feet.

Conversations about 'passing on the faith,' the changes in society, and the demise of Sunday School usually have a desperate undertone. We want to think that if we can just get the right curriculum, or hire the right director, or advertise better, or this, or that, or whatever . . . we can get back to the way things were.

It has never been a faithful way forward to spend your energy trying to recreate the past. The change in society, and what society values, causes a strong emotional response in grief and loss. And with no clear vision of what will become of the institution of the church, people feel a sense of desperation.

You may be hoping that I will now resolve the tension building in this chapter by offering you the perfect solution, "Here it is! Just send three easy payments of $9.99!" But there is no such solution. What I can offer you is this. At our best the church is a place of *authentic community* that includes *honest relationships, shared passion in service* and *mutual accountability*. If we spend our time on these instead of on being right, we will find our way forward.

For Further Reflection or Discussion

- What do you think of the author's assertion that much of our culture is searching for *authentic community*?

- Is the search for *authentic community* harder or easier for the affluent?

- Have you been a part of a group you would describe as *authentic community*?

- Is there a ministry in your church or community that happens a certain way "Because this is how we want to do it", or the more colloquial "that's the way we have always done it"? Is that *authentic community*?

- Where are places in your experience where desperation lies just below the surface of a normal encounter?

Scripture for further consideration
Read Luke 8:40-56

This is a story of a healing inside a story of a healing. It also appears in Matthew's Gospel, Matthew 9:18-26. As you read this story take note of the people Jesus encounters, and how desperate they are. What does their desperation cause them to do?

Prayer

Dear God, in all the places we are feeling desperate in our lives wash over us with your peace. In all the places we encounter desperate people, speak comfort and peace through us. And in all the ways you know we need, we pray that you will lead us into authentic community that is centered on you. In Jesus' Name, AMEN.

The Way Forward

CHAPTER 4

Stranger

I was a stranger and you welcomed me

Matt.25:35c

The Way Forward

I was 16 years old in the summer of 1985. I was active in my church youth group and the youth ministry of my denomination. That summer I was asked to be a representative at a youth symposium on the issues of hunger, homelessness and poverty in Washington, D.C. and New York. Traveling across the country alone and staying with a group of about 40 youth from around the country for two weeks was an adventure with many stories worth telling, but there is one evening in particular that will stick with me forever. During our time in Washington, D.C. there was an evening that a national church leader from our denomination came to speak to the teens from around the country gathered for this event. His talk was about getting outside our comfortable space and reaching out to those in need. He was really inspirational and afterward we were motivated. So much so, that a small group of us, four boys and four girls, left our hotel, a couple blocks from the National Mall, and set out to find "strangers." We were so jazzed about getting out into the world and helping others we went out and greeted tourists and foreigners and street people with equal enthusiasm. We encountered a few people near our hotel but as we got closer to the mall there were a couple blocks where we came across no one so we picked up our pace a bit. As we came to the mall, we rounded a corner to find an angry man standing over a woman whom he had apparently thrown down into the shrubs in front of an office building. He was yelling at her, threatening her, and he hit her a couple times before we could react. All together, emboldened by being a group, we started yelling for him to stop and rushed toward them. Startled, the man ran the other way. We helped the woman up and tried to comfort her. We heard the story of her immediate situation. She was homeless and had slept in these bushes the last couple of nights, but was specifically hiding from the man who had been threatening her. She told us he had raped her before, and she knew he would again any time he found her alone at night. So she was constantly hiding. As fairly sheltered kids from mostly suburban places, we were stunned by the plain way she described these things none of us had experienced, but only heard or read about. We tried to comfort her, and stepped away to put our heads together. Our situation was that we were two to a room, a queen bed each, staying in a hotel in a town we didn't know very well. We didn't know what resources were around or available, we didn't know any of this woman's backstory, but we knew we had to do something. The four girls in our group shared adjoining rooms, and four beds between them. The boys' rooms were across the hall. We decided we would offer this woman a bed for the night. We knew we couldn't do much more than that, we knew there might be risks, but we also knew we had to help somehow. We weren't offering her anything more than one night of safety and rest. It was what we had.

We asked her if she would like to come stay with us for the night. She accepted. She was grateful and yet seemed a little suspicious, but we really understood that. Who wouldn't be suspicious in that situation? So, we took her back to our hotel, we ordered pizza, and the girls started making friends with this woman the way girls do. We all crowded into one of the girls' rooms, sharing stories, laughing together, eating our fill, and having a good time. Before the night was over the girls had painted her nails, done her hair and had a full-on slumber party. They gave the woman her own bed, which she couldn't remember ever having; they kept the inner door between the girls' rooms open because it felt safer for everyone. The girls' outer doors were closed but the boys left the outer doors to their rooms across the hall cracked open; in case the girls needed help they wouldn't have to waste time knocking. Now it seems silly and maybe too chivalrous, but it felt right at the time.

In the morning we all got up early, the girls let their guest shower as long as she wanted, and even fixed her hair up again before she left. She was gracious and humble, she was grateful and thanked us in a subdued way that made it clear that she didn't know how to show her gratitude because she had nothing to give in return. We tried to receive her thanks graciously as well and tried to tell her that she had blessed us by letting us help her. It is a hard thing to put into words even as an adult. Anyway, our parting was mutual, and it was blessed.

It is interesting and important to note that the woman didn't steal from us, wouldn't take the money we offered her, and was gracious in all respects. Not the stereotype of a homeless person. There were also no expectations about the following night, and we were under no illusions about her life being made better. We know we didn't change her place in life or help with her problems. We just gave her one night of safety, a warm dry place to sleep, and maybe a little distraction from her reality. I don't remember her name, or if we even asked what it was. One of us probably did, but it wasn't important. We just wanted to help. Any satisfaction we felt however, was short lived.

We went down for breakfast with all the rest of the gathering participants and sat together as we ate. When breakfast was over there was a large group outing planned, but instead of gathering the group the adults in charge sent everyone back to their rooms with instructions to wait till they were called. Before the group disbanded they called out, by name, a small group who was to stay behind: the eight of us. We were asked into a smaller room where eight chairs sat in a row in front of two long tables where the adult leaders took seats. We were not trying to keep secret our hospitality from the previous night, but we hadn't been bragging about it either. It seems the adults in charge got wind of our hosting a homeless woman in our rooms over breakfast and were quite perturbed. None of the eight of us was very surprised; we knew we were doing something a little risky, but it had turned out fine. However, we were surprised, and shocked actually, at how angry the adults were. One by one they took turns giving us stern parental lecturing about responsibility and rules, and threatening to send us home. At a couple of points members of our group tried to respond with an explanation about how moved we were by the speaker from the night before, only to be shot down, or even yelled at. Finally, after our "reprimand" had lasted more than 40 minutes and the threatened consequence of our being sent home had been reiterated repeatedly, the pastor for the gathering addressed us. He was clearly angry and gave us a lecture (or more of a sermon) about "the sinfulness of disobedience" and used strong theological language to expound on how clearly sinful we were and in need of forgiveness. But in order to receive forgiveness we needed to repent!

We had sat, fairly compliant, taking what licks it seemed we needed to, for almost an hour. But, finally, I had had too much. Punishment is one thing, but using my faith and relationship with God to intimidate me with such clear hypocrisy pushed me over the edge. I stood up and stepped forward, took a long quiet breath, leaned over the table and pointed my finger at that pastor. "If what we did was a sin . . . then I will see you in hell." I said it strongly, but without raising my voice, then I turned and walked out. The rest of the group followed and went silently back to our rooms to await "sentencing." We all expected to be sent home. About half an hour later the whole gathering was called down to the lobby and continued with the outing planned for the morning. Not another word was spoken about the entire event. I've always wondered about that.

Even a few minutes after leaving that room, I would have admitted that it was not the most mature thing I could have done or said. In fact I don't even know how it came out that way, it just did. I was mad. Now, so many years later, I am sure that was not one of my finer moments. I am not proud of how I responded to those adults in authority, and I am also fairly certain I would probably respond the exact same way again, even now. I would like to think that, even as an adult, knowing more now about the dangers of the world than I did then, I would still put myself out there by helping a person in need. The solution eight teens came up with when faced with sexual violence and homelessness was short-lived, and didn't change anything. Or maybe it did. And even if it didn't, it has the potential.

What solutions can you imagine? What ways could you reach out to a person in need, even if only for one night? How might a tide of solitary acts change our world?

A profound experience sometimes happens when you have made space for it on purpose, and you engage in the experience with expectance. The following story does not sound as if it has to do with welcoming the stranger, but bear with me.

I was called to a church in the southwest. It was a place of great ministry and great potential but each ministry area had been allowed to function separately from the others for a long time. This had created "silos" of ministry that had turf, some degree of autonomy, and a leader or staff person dedicated just for that "silo." One example was the variety of programs that would fall in the category of 'adult education': Bible studies, adult forums, classes, retreats, and others. And sometimes there were people who participated in more than one but they were all led separately and the leaders paid little or no mind to what the other programs were doing. When asking questions about how we might collaborate I was even told once by a lay leader, "I don't care what THEY are doing, I am doing what I want to do!" There was a lot of "us and them" in that place. We would eventually get past it and create a healthier community. In addressing the silos I was reluctant to form an "education committee" or some other group for oversight. No one, including me, wanted one more committee meeting, although that is how these kinds of things have been handled in the past. Instead I worked to establish a relationship with the leader in each area. Soon enough there were three leaders, one woman and two men, with whom I established a good rapport. I invited them to join me for a book study, and specifically so we could study *A Generous Orthodoxy* by Brian McLaren. I also told them clearly that I hoped in growing relationships with each other some programmatic collaboration would organically grow out of our time together. So we began meeting every few weeks, reading and studying, using McLaren's book and scripture to direct our conversation. Eventually we moved on to another book by Brian McLaren, but our pattern was the same. We gathered, lit a candle, I opened in prayer, read the passage from the Bible, and we would launch into discussion. I tried hard to make my role in the group consistent by starting on time, and tying off the discussion at one hour. If any of them wanted to stay after and continue talking that was fine, but as a group we honored the time with good boundaries. Also, this really is intended to be dialog although pastors can often dominate and do more talking than others (or than they should), so I was purposeful about participating but not leading. To that end, when I finished reading the Bible passage I closed the book and didn't speak first. Often I waited until each person had offered something in the discussion before I joined or added anything. I really believe I have just as much to learn from them and wanted this to be dialog.

This was our pattern and it went very well. Our dialog was often passionate, our discussion was usually spirited, and our time together always included laughter. The four of us were respectful of each other, genuinely grew to like each other and eventually there were significant collaborative changes that grew out of these relationships. But our time together had more value in our relationship with each other than anything that came about in program leadership.

All of that background to tell you about this. We had been meeting for about a year when something profound happened in our gathering. We gathered the way we had become accustomed: start on time, candle, prayer, Bible reading. When I finished reading I closed the Bible and we sat in silence . . . for the whole hour.

We had not discussed it. We had not agreed ahead of time. It had not even been suggested that we take some quiet to reflect. It just happened. Four leaders, moved by the Spirit, sat in silent reflection for an hour! Let me be clear, we are four leaders, four alpha dogs, who are very capable of stepping in to lead a group if we sense that there is a lack or a need. This was not four wallflowers sitting awkwardly not knowing what to say, although in truth some of that hour felt awkward. And also in truth, I broke the silence twice during that hour. We had been sitting in silence for about 20 minutes when some louder conversation started up in the next office. It felt like a threat to our time so I opened the Bible and read the passage, out loud, again. I really thought that would draw us into discussion but the result was the same. By the time I had finished, the conversation in the next office was done and we stepped back into silence. The same thing happened at the 45-minute mark with the same result. At the hour mark I got out my calendar and asked when we should meet next and we ended our gathering as if we had been speaking the whole time, and none of us said anything about it!?! I spent the rest of my day scratching my head and wondering, "What the . . . ?"

Over the next week I found time to speak privately with each of them and took time to ask why. Why did you sit in silence? And why do you think the others did? One said "I was in a dark place personally and felt I had nothing to offer. And I have no idea why the others did." Another said, "I look for opportunities for meditation everywhere. Maybe we each were afraid to break the silence of the others." And the other said, "I was responding to the invitation I heard implied in the text to 'be still'. I think we needed it."

We live in a world that seems to despise quiet, and forcefully rejects the notion of silence. You probably only need ponder for a second to identify the loud noises in your life that demand to be heard all the time. And I'm sure that, like me, you can think of friends or acquaintances who can't sit still or hold silence for ten seconds without checking their phone or filling the void. Yet there we sat, for an hour, not just being silent but holding the silence of each other. In this time when real and honest relationships are a precious commodity there are still those places where we can know and be known by others. We started this group as little more than strangers, but in time, by purposeful intent, we became deeply connected.

In our finer moments, when we are not wrangling over music and mission statements, our communities of faith are the places where real relationship happens. When Jesus said in his parable, "I was a stranger and you invited me in" (Matt. 25:35c) I think he meant for us to start with each other, and it will grow from there.

It has been said that Sunday morning is the most segregated few hours of the week. And more than just race, our churches are largely homogenous in politics, age, socio-economics, etc.. It seems we are terrible at "welcoming the stranger" unless that new person walks and talks like us. I don't think most Christians today want this to be the case. We want young people, we want old people, we want people of other orientations and ethnicities to be a part of our fellowship. But we are stuck; we have been doing what is comfortable for so long I don't think we know how to welcome a stranger.

One of the gems of wisdom that came out of the "church growth movement" of the early 1990s is really helpful. In all the ways our conventional wisdom would say, a good youth program, or modern music, or dynamic preaching are what make a healthy growing church, they are all wrong. While small group ministry and prayer teams may be meaningful, and all these things can be good, they are not what makes a healthy vibrant congregation.

The single greatest factor is this: a caring community. When people step in the door, do they see a gathering of people who care for one another, and does it appear they care at all about me. At the same moment it is much more complicated than 'feeling welcome,' it is also so much easier than programs and personnel. And you can't fake it. Either your congregation is a caring community or it is not. But here is the most amazing part: the culture of a place can be changed by one person. One person can make up their mind to turn to the person sitting nearest them on Sunday morning and ask them how they are, and really listen to the answer. Really listening to one another, and caring as much for the other person's side of the conversation as we do for our own is hard work, but worth it. Things won't change overnight, and it may be true that some places will always be selfish and self-centered, but nothing changes without work. Before long, you will realize that by turning to a person each week, asking and listening, you'll be surprised how many strangers you meet.

For Further Reflection or Discussion

- Have you ever seen first-hand the reality of living on the street? Where? When?

- What are some of the complicating realities when we are dealing with homelessness?

- Where have you seen hypocrisy in leadership? How have you responded? Or have you?

- Have you ever sat in silent reflection, for any amount of time, on purpose? What was it like?

- When was the last time you talked with a person you didn't know? How did it start?

Scripture for further consideration
Read Luke 10:25-37

This story is usually called "The Parable of the Good Samaritan" and is unique to Luke's Gospel. The context is a teacher of the law coming to "test" Jesus. Jesus' response to the test, is to tell a story. Samaritans were despised by Jews and so the characters of this story are shamed by the actions of "the one who showed mercy." So much so, that the teacher of the law can't even bring himself to name "the Samaritan" as the one who showed mercy.

Prayer

Dear God, help us to live out our faith as if there are no strangers in the world, only friends we haven't met yet. When we encounter those who are different from us may we first see the diversity of your creation and give thanks, rather than highlighting our differences. And may we be instruments that bring about your peace. In Jesus' Name, AMEN.

CHAPTER 5

Naked

I was naked and you gave me clothing

Matt.25:36a

When my wife and I were first married we lived in Spokane, Washington, in an old neighborhood called "The Browne's Addition." I liked riding my mountain bike around town, and on trails. The Spokane River runs along the edge of the neighborhood and there is a steep hill that goes down to it. One summer afternoon I decided to see what was down along the river. I rode my mountain bike down the hill and found some good trails that looked as if they went toward the river. They did.

I rode for a while along the trails. It was quiet, and fun riding. I had been riding for a while when I passed a man walking the other way. I encountered him a bit suddenly and had passed around him before I realized . . . he was naked. He was quite fat and obviously not wearing a shirt, but naked? I looked back over my shoulder, and sure enough, the view from behind revealed the truth. (Pun intended!) That big guy was buck-naked! I stopped for a moment and thought about going back to ask him if he was okay or needed help, but he had barely even acknowledged me, and had kept trundling right on up the path. I rode on a while, pondering and confused, then came to the river. The trail I was on came out on a large flat beach area right along the river. Right away I was very surprised by how many people were on this beach. I had only seen the one man on the trail, and it had been a quiet peaceful trail, but here were some fifty people out on this beach. I was also further surprised to realize none of them was wearing any clothes.

I'm not a prude. I know what a nude beach is, and I think I know why people would go there, and further, I am okay with it. Only, I had never been to one, and I guess I thought they were something you found in Europe or foreign countries, or at least California. But not anywhere I lived. I was totally shocked.

I stood there at the edge of the trees, astride my bike, staring out at the 50 or so people on the beach for what was probably an embarrassingly long time, gawking. I didn't care, and no one even noticed me standing there. I had a hard time processing what I was seeing, and it was a spectacle that was hard to look away from, sad as that is to admit. And here is the part that surprised me the most. There was not one person there who looked like a supermodel. I was in my mid-20s and if you had asked me what a nude beach looked like I would have assumed it looked like a Victoria's Secret catalog, only better. This was not. Every person on that beach was either really old and saggy, or huge, or both. Once I realized what I had stumbled on, I looked closely. (Again, sad to admit.) And here is an important truth for living that is hard for anyone to learn without doing: once you've looked, you can't un-look.

As I rode away from that beach, I was amazed at how differently I saw the world. I'm not sure that I saw people differently, but I realized I had some sort of idealized view of the world, and that had changed. It was as if I had stumbled across a unicorn out in the woods and found that it was just a malformed billy-goat. We idealize many things in our minds, but how much of that is really concocted fantasy? I have wondered that ever since.

When I think of the words of Jesus' parable, his commission that we should 'clothe the naked,' I think back on my experience along the Spokane River. What if those who are naked are that way because they want to be? Should I have walked around that day asking if anyone wanted my shirt? It is a childish way to address Jesus' commission, especially when there truly are those in our communities, and our world, who are in real need of clothing. At the same time we need to acknowledge that there are those in our community who will choose to be naked, or choose to be homeless, or choose to refuse the help they are offered. What do we do with that? The first answer is that we don't stop offering, or stop working, or give up in any way. It also means that we have to open our eyes and our hearts to see the truth; not every homeless person sleeps on the street, not every hungry person lacks food, and not every naked person lacks clothing.

I served for more than a decade at a church in the suburbs of Portland, Oregon. One day I was working alone in my office in the middle of the afternoon. Everyone else had gone for the day. There was a knock on the outside door, and when I went to answer it there was woman in her mid-20s with large sunglasses and a plastic bag from a department store in her hands. It looked as if she had just been shopping at the mall. Maybe she is inquiring about the church preschool, or looking for someone, or as is commonly in the back of my mind, maybe she is panhandling. I open the door and greet her, and all my preconceptions are shot. She speaks clearly, but there is a slight tremble in her voice. "Will you please help me? I am trying to get away from a man who beats me. I have been turned away from three other churches, and I am walking. If I can't get help soon I will have to go back before he gets home from work or it will be worse. Will you please help me? I don't want to go back." And it's then that I notice the large gaudy sunglasses are hiding a largely swollen face, and I realize the plastic bag has just what was necessary for her to bring. She left everything else behind.

That was the beginning of an odyssey that lasted the rest of the day, and has bothered me deeply ever since. I had never dealt with the reality of domestic violence so personally. I have to admit that I responded with a very paternal instinct. I knew immediately this woman was telling the truth, and that I would do anything within my power to help her.

As we were trying to find her resources and help she shared more of her story with me. She had been living with this man for about three years and everything was great for a while. Then there were small episodes of abuse. Eventually they grew more frequent, and recently they had been constant. She had been making a plan to leave for some time, she had made contact with a relative who she could stay with, and the following weekend was to be her escape. But the last three days had been the worst ever. She described being beaten for hours each night, and the previous night he had held her up against a wall by her throat till she was nearly unconscious, then thrown her across the room. She was afraid she would not live till the weekend.

Together we tried to access resources in the greater Portland area that could help in her situation. After hours on the phone, many conversations with social workers, and searching every crack or cranny of the social services agencies that might have help, we had only a sad education to show for it.

There are more than two million people living in the Portland metro area. There are thousands of KNOWN situations of ongoing domestic violence. And the number of beds available in shelters that can help women get out of those situations numbers only in the dozens! There are hundreds of women on waiting lists for the minuscule resources that are available.

It was like falling down a rabbit hole in 'Alice in Wonderland.' The labyrinth of apparent services available seemed to have promising turns along the way but an evil twist at the end of each path. After working so hard to find a way through, the maze actually led back to the beginning. Going home to the abuser was actually proposed as a better alternative to life on the street.

Late in the day I made a call to a friend who is a social worker at a family shelter in the area. I explained the situation and she was very kind in explaining to me that there were essentially no services available to someone in this situation. Then at the end, and because she is my friend and knows me, she said, "And, no matter what happens, do not take her home with you!"

I had already resolved to do that very thing if we could find no other options. We had a spare room, and I knew my wife would have welcomed this woman into our home and wrapped her in love and kindness. In fact I had already asked her, so I knew she would. But my friend was right, without skilled clinical evaluation there would be no way of knowing what I would be exposing my wife, children and even my neighbors to. No matter how much information I had gotten from this woman, these situations are always more complicated. And the truth is we didn't have the skill, knowledge or experience to deal with any of the complications we knew about, let alone the ones we didn't.

In the end we found another answer. My church did not have much in the way of funds to help with rent, utilities, or needs like that. But I was able to negotiate with a low-end motel in a neighboring suburb for a cheap rate that I would find funds to take care of for the three nights this woman needed until she could move in with her relative. I drove her there myself and further negotiated with the manager to make sure she would be well treated. I gave her what little money I had in my wallet for food, and I asked her to stay in touch and let me know how things worked out, and if she needed help again to call. She was very grateful and called me the following day to let me know she had followed up with some of the county resources for counseling but that was still going to take a while. Then I didn't hear from her again. She checked out of the motel on the last morning, and I hope she left to begin a new life. But I may never know.

This young woman had little more than the clothes on her back. But she had clothes. And to look at her as you passed on the street you would not notice that she was in need of clothing, but she was. She was desperately in need of the basic clothing of safety. When the king in Jesus' parable says "I needed clothes and you clothed me" (Matt. 25:36a) I know this means more than shirts and shoes. Clothing those in need is not just sending supplies to needy people in third world countries, it is clothing those in need in our very midst.

There are no easy answers to the problems of our society, and the difficulty of those problems can feel overwhelming. There are just as many reasons not to get involved as there are to help, but our call as people of faith is to care for others, all others. I don't offer easy answers. I am not even sure I can articulate the questions before us so they make sense. But we must move forward into the uncertainty, using our limited resources and our best efforts, even when they feel inadequate and feeble. We live into a new reality where not every homeless person sleeps on the street, not every hungry person lacks food, and not every naked person lacks clothing.

For the last few years I have lived in Tucson, Arizona. Tucson is in Pima County, and the Pima County Board of Supervisors is the legislative authority there. In 2016 the Board of Supervisors passed an ordinance making it illegal to loiter on the median of a road. The ordinance goes so far as to define such loitering as being at the median for more than one cycle of the traffic lights.

Clearly this is an ordinance aimed at removing panhandlers who are doing what is known on the streets as "flying a sign." I am sure every metro area in the country has had to deal with people begging by the side of the road, usually holding a sign scrawled on cardboard. And I am sure there are other places that have tried to address it by making laws like this. While lawmakers might claim these laws address issues of "public safety" or "financial liability," those are excuses that mask the underlying motivation. Laws like these are largely motivated by the selfish desire to move the reality of poverty out of the way so I don't have to look at it. Our society, and most specifically the wealthy part of our society, doesn't like seeing the poor, or in any way being made to feel guilty. Being looked at by a beggar while stopped at a traffic light can feel awkward and uncomfortable, but if we really ask why we feel that way it has nothing to do with public safety.

In a bid for re-election one of those supervisors in Pima County used yard signs that claimed this individual had "Got panhandlers off our streets!" Some of those signs were posted along major intersections, I can only assume to emphasize the point. A more truthful sign would have read, "Trying to make poverty illegal, or at least invisible!" If the panhandlers are "off our streets," where did we put them?

When we spend our time and resources making laws about sleeping on sidewalks, handing out food in the park, or roadside begging, we are attempting to avoid working on what is actually ailing our society. The issues of poverty in our society are large, complex and often systemic. Addressing these issues is hard work and sometimes unpopular. Seeking to remove evidence of poverty in our community, making it harder to see, actually adds to the difficulty of addressing it. Wouldn't it be great if our elected leaders worked as hard on issues of poverty as they did on getting re-elected?

I seldom give money to those who are panhandling, but I certainly do not fault people who do. It may seem as if the obvious need is for money, but it is really not the case. Lack of money is not what brings a person to beg on the street corner or off-ramp. Whether they're on the street because of addiction or mental illness or some other major factor, simply adding money to their situation will not fix it. I work in other areas of my life to bring about change that will help the larger situation of our society, the issues of poverty specifically, and I give to organizations that do that work as well. To address the immediate need, I carry granola bars around in my glovebox and give them out as often as asked.

The more we spend building walls, the harder it is to see our neighbor. The more we fool ourselves into thinking gated communities are safer, the harder it is to see our neighbor. When we avoid seeing our neighbor, we avoid seeing the needs of our neighbor. We must open our eyes wider and not deny the realities that need changing in our world. To do that requires us to also open our hearts. It is easy to fool ourselves and rationalize not caring for others, and even more so when we separate ourselves from what some find to be unpleasant realities of our world. "Out of sight, out of mind." But God cares as much for our neighbor as for us, and so should we. When we see a naked person it might be our tendency to avert our eyes. Do we do the same when we see a person in need?

As I said earlier in this chapter, not every homeless person sleeps on the street, not every hungry person lacks food, and not every naked person lacks clothing, but some do, so let's get to work.

For Further Reflection or Discussion

- Why do you think we have the cultural norms and convictions about nudity that we do?

- What do you think of the author's statement "not every homeless person sleeps on the street, not every hungry person lacks food, and not every naked person lacks clothing"?

- Why do you think there is such a lack of resources for those in situations of domestic violence? How can your church get involved?

- Why do you think we tend towards quick, easy solutions rather than address the underlying causes of our social issues?

- How can you help motivate our leaders to address the real needs in our society?

Scripture for further consideration
Read John 8:2-11

This story is unique to John's Gospel and is usually called "the woman caught in adultery." Notably, we never hear about a man caught in adultery, but clearly the woman wasn't acting alone. It is hard to speak truth to power, but clearly it is needed in every generation.

Prayer

Dear God, give us courage to speak out when we see violence in our community. Give us courage to speak out when we see gender inequity. Give us courage to speak out as people of faith. In Jesus' Name, AMEN.

CHAPTER 6

Sick

I was sick and you took care of me.

Matt.25:36b

I'm sitting on the back porch of the main lodge at camp, looking out through the trees toward the parking lot. In a few minutes the retreat groups from churches around my home town will be finishing lunch in the dining hall, gathering at their vehicles and loading up for home. It will be simple to hitch a ride with one of them.

I have been at this camp for two weeks. Three months ago when I was filling out the employment application in my dorm room I thought it would be the most perfect and amazing summer job, but things have not worked out the way I thought they would. The first ten days were staff training, and each day we learned about safety things, or procedures for how things run at this camp, and a huge variety of other things. And each night we took turns in small groups leading the others in songs, games, skits, campfire activities or other things we would need to do with the kids we would work with during the summer. And it was a fun, silly way of bonding together as a staff. There are some amazing, outgoing, creative, hilarious people on this staff. I am not one of them.

In front of groups I feel awkward, when I am trying to be funny no one laughs, I am not cool like the other people on this staff, and I can't think on my feet with activities, games and the other things camp counselors are supposed to do with kids at summer camp. This has been way too apparent the last three days. As the 'first try' at using the things we learned in staff training we start the summer with a three-day high school retreat. High school youth groups from all around the region, some from my home town, have been here for a long three-day weekend retreat. The boys in my cabin were loud, they were obnoxious around other groups, they were rude at meals and at campfires, they didn't do what I told them to do, and they would not shut up at night. It feels like I haven't had five minutes of sleep for the last three days. Things went so badly with my very first opportunity to be a 'camp counselor', the only success I can see is that none of my campers was injured or died while I was in charge. Not really what I would call a smashing success. Now that the first retreat group is leaving, so am I. They leave at lunch, and a whole new group of campers will be here by dinner, only that group will be here for a whole week. I want to be gone before they get here.

My packed bag sits next to me, and I am trying, yet again, to finger some chords on this stupid guitar. I have been hauling this guitar around for weeks and no amount of time spent practicing seems to make any difference. I ought to just leave it right here on the porch when I go. It might make it easier to get a ride if I have less baggage. I've just resolved to abandon my guitar and leave a note that says "free," when Monica walks around the corner.

I have known Monica for a few years. She grew up in a neighboring town and during high school our church youth groups had started doing stuff together. She is a couple of years younger than me, and this weekend has come along as a helper with her church's youth group because she has been out of high school for a year. Monica is tall, slender and beautiful, but socially awkward. Her parents pushed her to be a figure skater for most of her younger life, insisted on perfect grades, and had sent her to some sort of finishing-school type of training they made her do privately. As a result she has insanely perfect posture and balance (it seems in all situations), she has impeccable manners (also in all situations), and she is wicked smart. She can have proper and polite conversation with adults, but her ability to interact with her peers is always very stiff and stilted. She is beautiful, friendly and nice, but hard to talk with.

She comes around the corner and says, "There you are! I've been looking all over for you." I can't imagine why, but here might be my opportunity to find a ride. She has an agenda however, and before I can formulate my request she blazes ahead.

"I have been trying all weekend to find a time to say thank you for saving my life." Stunned, I can't imagine what in the world she is talking about. "What?" is the only word I can find. After a moment of looking at me intensely, she begins with something she must have practiced because it comes out far more smooth and direct than she normally speaks. Still stunned, I just listen. "Several years ago I had decided to kill myself. My parents had been pushing me really hard with my skating and I resented it. I was so sick of skating I had begun to hate it. But my parents were so invested and demanding, I couldn't see any way forward that didn't devastate and disappoint them. And I thought if they were disappointed in me they wouldn't love me. I didn't have any friends because I spent so much time skating, and had to study so hard in order to get perfect grades, I just felt so alone. I was alone. I couldn't imagine a future that didn't include skating, and by then I hated everything about skating. I made up my mind. The only way out was to end my life. I made a plan and picked a date, but the weekend before I had planned, the youth leader at my church convinced my parents to send me with our youth group to the retreat that was at your church. When our group arrived at your church you were the first person we met. Your youth group was in the middle of a running game on the lawn in front of your church. And when we drove up you greeted us, invited us to join the game, then you took my hand and pulled me into the game. For the rest of the weekend you and your friends treated me like I was part of the group. No one had ever treated me like that before. No one had ever loved me like that before. By the end of the weekend I knew I could never go through with my plan. I saw my life differently by the time I got home. Our youth groups have done so many things together since then, and every time I am with you, I see the same love for others that changed my life. I've seen it all weekend at this retreat, so I know it's not just for me." Then she looks me square in the face with intensity and says, "Thank you for saving my life."

I stammer. I don't know what to say. I open and shut my mouth a couple times, unable to even form words in response. I struggle for a bit, then she grabs me up in a hug around the neck so hard it chokes me. A really long hug. When she lets go, she turns and walks away, hustling off to go help her group load up. Clearly she didn't really want a response, she just wanted me to know.

I sit on the porch on the back of the lodge for a long time, staring out through the trees toward the parking lot, until the lot is empty and everyone has gone. Eventually I pick up my bag . . . and my guitar . . . and head back up the hill to camp. I have a cabin to clean; campers will be arriving soon.

As I have reflected on that day I continue to be moved and humbled. Try as I might, I can not remember the day I first met Monica. I have never doubted her story; how could I? But what changed her life wasn't even a memory for me. That scares the crap out of me. What if I had been having a bad day? What if I had gone to the movies instead of youth group that night? What if I had been sick? What if, What if, What if?

She was sick, and I didn't know it. The only thing that "*looked after*" her when she was sick, was being welcomed and included. It wasn't medicine, bedside manner, or pastoral visitation. How was I to know that welcoming and including another kid in a game would heal them? I was a kid myself!?!

And it also occurs to me, I wonder if she knew I was sick and in need of "*looking after*"? That day on the porch, looking out toward the parking lot, looking for a ride to somewhere else, I needed healing and encouragement. Maybe she knew it. She always was smarter than me.

Do we get visions of hospitals, doctors and nurses when we think of "I was sick and you looked after me"(Matt. 25:36b)? There are many, many sicknesses that hospitals don't treat. When we hear Jesus' commission to care for the sick, we really should add the words 'in all ways' after it. There are so many ways we can care for others that are healing and life-giving that don't involve medicine. In caring for those we meet or encounter, even if it is just once, we are living in a way that provides healing in our world and in the lives of others.

I have a friend, a colleague and retired pastor, who is the most joy filled and humble example of a human being I have ever known. I have known him for over ten years and have known him in good times and bad.

When I first met Louie in 2003, he had been a retired pastor for a long time. Along the way he was given the title of "pastor emeritus" by his last congregation, of which he had remained a member. In all of my experience, everyone who met Louie knew right away that he loved his wife with a deep and abiding love. He was her primary care provider and had been for a long time.

In 1971 Glenna had been diagnosed with multiple sclerosis, and although their life changed drastically, they were able to lead a fairly normal life. They raised four kids, served together in ministry, and were actively engaged in life. In 1981 Glenna had a grand mal seizure and they learned she had viral encephalitis. The result was a large loss of cognitive ability, some of which she never got back. They continued in ministry until 1993 when Louie "retired." (He continued to do visitation ministry for his congregation, and worked in a more voluntary ministry for several years.) In retirement Louie and Glenna traveled extensively, spent as much time as they could with family, and stayed as active as they were able. During that time Glenna was mostly confined to a wheelchair and Louie cared for her, transported her, and transferred her from bed to wheelchair to car and back again, everywhere she needed to go. As Glenna declined, and Louie grew older, he grew ever more crafty in fashioning ways to transfer Glenna from one seat to another. Most notably, he created a notched wooden ramp that secured her wheelchair to the doorframe of the car, making it possible for him to transfer her in and out of the passenger seat without assistance. On many occasions I witnessed them coming and going at various gatherings, often in the rain. Regularly I would offer to help with the transfer to or from the car, occasionally my help was accepted, but never once did Louie complain or allow the hardship to dampen his spirits. Many were the times when my colleagues and I would remark on this, always noting that we frequently allow our moods to darken when we experience far less struggle. Louie maintains a positive outlook and a joyful spirit in the midst of struggles that would devastate our outlook. And he is not faking it. He, and Glenna, really have that much joy in their hearts.

Louie took Glenna everywhere. Not just traveling, but to ministry conferences, family gatherings, church events, cruises and everything they would have done before. And when it was difficult, he found a way. When I met Louie and Glenna in 2003 Glenna was alert, but not cognitively able to converse or engage. And even still, when greeted, she would shake your hand and beam with joy at meeting you, whoever you were, as though you had been friends for years.

I have seen that when dementia, or some other cognitive impairment, diminishes a person's capacity, often times a deep layer of their character is revealed. For some that is fear or anger, but for Glenna it was joy, real and true joy that you could tell was genuine, to her very core. Even in her last days, she was glad to meet you, whoever you were, and for whatever reason.

I only knew Glenna in this last stage. I knew nothing of her glorious singing voice, or her laughter at family and church social gatherings, and never had a conversation with her. I only knew her joy at greeting, and the obvious deep and abiding love she and Louie shared.

There were times when Louie would bring Glenna along when he would attend overnight events with other pastors and their spouses, and I don't know anyone who ever heard Louie complain. In fact, just the opposite. Even on the worst day of struggle or hardship, Louie was thankful, gracious, generous, kind and joyful. (Note: "joyful" is not the same as "happy.") I know he would never agree to my assessment, because he feels struggles like we all do. But even in the midst of struggle it is in his nature to be thankful and see God's grace in his life, and the lives of those around him. Many of us who were around Louie and Glenna during that time saw them struggle, offered help that was accepted, and saw that there was no "veneer of positive thinking" or falseness to the way Louie and Glenna were. They were really thankful and joyful, even in hardship.

In every photo of Louie and Glenna, on cruises, with family, and at church gatherings, they are both smiling with their whole face, as if the camera caught them in mid-laughter. They seemed to smile so hard you thought their head might split open from the exuberance, and it was genuine every time.

For me, when Jesus says "I was sick and you looked after me" (Matt. 25:36b), the vision of Louie caring for Glenna will always move me deeply. There are so many times we celebrate with people at their weddings, and hear them declare *"in sickness and in health, till death do us part."* And so many of those times, when tested, they renege. But on rare occasions we get a glimpse of who we aspire to be. I pray that if I am ever tested with similar challenges, instead of the darker things I know I have inside, the joy in my life will be revealed.

I have attended many funerals. And in those occasions a simple observation is that most family's grief reveals their emotional and spiritual health, or lack of it, both as individuals and as a family. Most remarkably, I have never attended a funeral like Glenna's.

Several family members spoke, a couple performed music, and there was the typical litany, prayers and scripture readings one would expect from a Protestant memorial service. What made this an unusual experience for me was the joy with which the family spoke, and the constancy with which they expressed their faith. In the service time and in the conversations afterward there was a mesmerizing consistency. There were tears and emotion expressed, don't hear me saying it was all laughter and levity. There were highs and lows in the sharing, but the depth and honest joy with each was remarkable. (As I noted earlier, joy and happiness are not the same thing. We often mistake them.)

Cynically a person might say, "Well, they are a family who know how to put up a good front." But that would be a cynic who hadn't ever met Louie and Glenna together. This wasn't a family episode from the 700 Club. There was no broadcast and there was nothing to be gained from any of it. Instead it was the most healthy, and honest, celebration of a life by a family of faith that I have ever witnessed.

Even a person who didn't know Glenna could see evidence of healthy relationships and a family that share a deep and abiding faith. That by itself gives witness to genuine faith and joy that define Louie and Glenna as people.

I share this story of Louie and Glenna long after Glenna has passed away. And still the evidence of the joyful loving exuberance of life is evident in anyone who recalls meeting the two of them together. Louie gave me his permission to share this story, and his blessing in my writing. But he has given me far more blessing in modeling the kind of person I can only hope to be. It is obvious to me that there are a myriad of ways a person can be sick and in need of healing, and many of those illnesses are not obvious from the outside. But if we can start by attempting to care for the illness we can see, our intention will spill over and work healing in what we can't see. Thank you, Louie.

Our commission to care for the sick will always take different forms. We may not be called on to care for the ailing parent, spouse or loved one. Or maybe we will. And there are many more ways that we can care for the sicknesses hidden in each of us. As the church, 'caring for the sick' has always been a priority for us. From founding hospitals to outreach ministries to parish nurses, we have found ways to care for those who are in need of healing. As we move into an uncertain time, what are ways that you, and your church, can focus your resources and energy on caring for the sick? What are ways that you, and your church, already are? How can you do it more? And when pushed by adversity, will the adversity reveal joy in your serving?

For Further Reflection or Discussion

- Have you ever been profoundly affected by what someone else did? Does that person know it?
- What are some sicknesses in our world that you can't see from the outside?
- Have you ever known a couple whose marriage is an inspiration for you?
- If you were ever to suffer from dementia, what part of your character would be revealed? What do you hope would be revealed?
- What is the difference between joy and happiness?

Scripture for further consideration
Read Acts 6:8-15

Stephen is a disciple we only hear about in this part of the book of Acts. In 6:1-7 he is chosen to be one of the seven in charge of caring for the needy. God continues to do great things through Stephen and he is arrested and put on trial. But even being falsely accused, Stephen still exudes goodness. They describe it by saying he has "the face of an angel." Chapter 7 is a long sermon Stephen gives to defend himself, but in the end, the leaders refuse to listen and kill Stephen by stoning him.

Prayer

Dear God, may even the smallest of our actions be used by you in sharing love to others. Even when we are rejected, we pray that you will give us the grace to stand firm in following you. And when we are tested may it reveal goodness IN us that represents your goodness TO us. In Jesus' Name, AMEN.

CHAPTER 7

Imprisoned

I was in prison and you visited me
Matt.25:36c

Sometimes at a church people will come in asking for help or assistance. Usually they are asking for money and it can be hard to discern true need from "panhandling." It happens often enough that, working in a church, a person can get a bit jaded about people who come in asking for a handout. At the very least it is hard to be patient. Church workers, both volunteer and professional, desire to help others and are often seen as easy marks for manipulation. Many are the occasions when I, or those I work with, have been cursed and ranted at by a drunk or strung out person. It is hard to maintain a compassionate attitude when you have been called many versions of "un-Christian" because you are unwilling to give out cash when it is demanded. It is hard not to become jaded. Most churches are ill equipped and unable to provide the assistance that is truly needed by most seeking money, but every church has referral agencies in their community that can provide aid with rent, utilities, shelter and food. Every church tries to help those who ask; some are better at it than others.

One day, while I was working in the church office, a man came in and asked to speak with the pastor. He wouldn't say why, he just needed to speak with the pastor. I try to make myself available for anyone who drops in, which means that I frequently deal with strangers who come in with a variety of needs. Some we can help, some we can't. When I met this particular man in the hallway outside my office I immediately jumped to the conclusion that he would be asking me for money. He was in his 40s, average build, average dress, and he said he wanted to speak just with me. Often that means I am about to hear a hard-luck story designed to guilt me into giving out money. (Remember, I used the word 'jaded'?) Well, I sized up this man . . . and I sized him up wrong.

We stepped into my office, I politely invited him to sit down, and he told me the following story.

"A long time ago a friend and I were driving past your church. Even back then the road in front of your church was busy. As we drove by, my friend, who was a cement worker by trade, saw a tool lying near the sidewalk next to your church. We both recognized it as a cement-working tool. My friend was driving, so he pulled over and told me to jump out and grab it. We both just assumed it had fallen off a worker's truck as he was driving by. Debris by the side of the road is usually fair game. I jumped out of my friend's truck and ran across the street and retrieved the tool. I picked it up and as I turned, I slipped in the edge of wet cement. All in the rush of a moment I realized I was stealing a tool someone was using, but had stepped away from their job for some reason. I did not mean to steal someone's tool, and felt guilty and scared all at the same time. Standing there in the street, with traffic coming, I panicked. I looked to my friend and I saw the same panic on his face because he had realized the same thing in the same moment. He yelled, 'Quick, get in the truck!' I jumped in the truck and we drove off fast. My friend and I never talked about that moment again, but I have thought about it every day since. I am here to pay the church back for that tool, and to ask for forgiveness."

I was a bit dumbfounded. Obviously my preconceived bias was dead wrong. As I was listening to his story I was trying to figure out when the last time someone would have been doing cement work beside the church and I knew with certainty it had been more than ten years. Later I would discover it had been way longer than that. I immediately realized this as one of those rare occasions that a person needs the formal declaration of forgiveness. I said, "You are forgiven. On behalf of the church, and God, I am here to tell you that you are forgiven." As the man pulled out a $100 bill I tried to refuse his money and explain that he did not need to pay for forgiveness. His confession was more than adequate. The man smiled and said "Pastor, I am Catholic, but even I know that's not the way it works. I'm not buying my forgiveness, I am making a donation to pay for the tool I took, even if there is no way of knowing whose it was." We prayed together, I told him again that he was forgiven, and I walked him out. As he was leaving, in the hall outside my office, he turned to me and said, "Like I said, I'm Catholic, so I know how it works with you guys; pastors and priests. Confidentiality and all that. But I give you my permission to tell this story if you think someone else would benefit from it. Just don't use my name." Then he left without another word, and I immediately, and purposefully forgot his name so I would never risk saying it, even by accident. And, truth be told, I would tell his story to others without his permission (and of course not use his name), but it was a very thoughtful gift for him to add. Clearly he had put a lot of thought into coming to my office, and it had weighed on him heavily.

It is actually overwhelming to think about. This man had been carrying this daily burden of guilt for well over a decade. How heavy a burden. How huge a debt in his mind. How hard it must have been for him to finally resolve to seek forgiveness. How many of us are carrying guilty burdens that have weighed us down for years? And how many of the people we encounter every day are carrying burdens like these?

It doesn't take concrete walls with bars on the windows to be a prison. Many people are living imprisoned with burdens that we have the power to release them from. And you don't have to be a representative of a church to free a person from their bondage. Each of us has the power in our own lives to free others, or at least walk alongside of them in their burdens. It is true that some people choose their burden, or lack the ability to let loose of it. But if we take the opportunity to speak forgiveness, to live with gratitude, and to be real with others, there is opportunity for freedom.

Here there are two really challenging tasks: looking honestly at our own burdens and being willing to honestly see the burdens of others. Sometimes we look the other way, we are unwilling to admit our own faults and burdens, and we refuse to see the burdens of others. Admitting our own struggles doesn't mean we are weak or inadequate. And it is only in admitting them that we can begin to lay them down, find resolution, or seek the forgiveness we need from others. The same is true for the other people in our lives. We have the power to help those around us by walking along side them, finding those opportunities to lighten their load with a kind word, honest companionship, or even the bold speaking of forgiveness.

You don't have to go through a security check point, metal detector, or pat-down to visit someone who is imprisoned. Although if you have the opportunity to visit a person in an actual prison, I hope you take it. There are so many places, and even daily opportunities to "visit the imprisoned."

My friend, Barbara Rintala, who has generously offered me her editorial skills in working on this book, shared the following story in a small group book study. She graciously is allowing me to share it here.

Salt and Light

I walked out of my apartment at 16th and New Hampshire at noon to catch the bus. My college roommate and her husband and I had agreed to meet near the National Mall for the event. As I rode downtown looking out the window of the bus, I was surprised to see something I had never seen before: the streets and sidewalks were almost empty. I thought that people must be afraid there would be violence. I wondered if anyone else would be there. I arrived, found my friends, and we walked over to the Mall.

The date was August 28, 1963. The event was the Great March on Washington for civil rights. The size of the crowd was later estimated at about 250,000.

From our place near the Washington Monument, we listened to a number of speakers who stood in front of the statue of Abraham Lincoln on the floor of the Lincoln Memorial, about a mile away. The sound system had been sabotaged the previous day, but was rebuilt overnight by the U.S. Army Signal Corps. And then finally the one we had been waiting for came to the microphone and began to speak. Dr. Martin Luther King, Jr. called eloquently for an end to racism in this country and ended his speech by describing his dream.

Dr. King articulated the dream we all had, a dream we hoped would come true. Under the spell of his words, the huge crowd became a community of brothers and sisters, gathered together by a single purpose. There was a feeling of inexpressible peace. That day was how it was supposed to be. That day was beautiful. Five years later Martin Luther King was shot and died at the age of 39. But you can't murder a dream.

As I look back on that day, it seems that for those few hours, in that place, the meek had inherited the earth, that justice could roll down like waters and righteousness like a mighty stream, that the kingdom of God had become visible among us, its light shining brightly in the midst of our battered and broken world.

This is Barbara's story. And what I hear in her story is the personal expression of the motive behind the civil rights movement. Our country had become little more than a prison for those who were not white. A prison with no walls or bars, but a prison all the same. The motive of the civil rights movement was to free the imprisoned. And a young white woman in the 60's participating in the Great March on Washington was most remarkably visiting the imprisoned.

Now today there is a new prison in our midst. The prison of fear that keeps the undocumented immigrant living in fear of the "justice system." All of us, save the native population (whom we actually believe to be a conquered people so we treat them as such), were at one time immigrants to this land. And now those who don't have the right slip of paper, and many of the citizens who do, are living in fear because of a new uprising of bigotry. Rather than do the work of engaging in relationship, rather than open our hearts and ask why they are here and listen to their story, and rather than share out of our excess (which we all have), we choose to imprison those we see as different, less, and other than we are. It is a command from our creator that we care for others, and even visit those who are in prison, but instead we choose to build larger prisons of hatred and fear.

If we are looking for the way forward, if we are following the trail markers of those who have come before us in faith, then we have to see that every time people have followed the path of hatred, demonizing others, fostering fear and building walls, it has led to destruction, not wholeness. Jesus' story in Matthew 25 is about God being pleased when we care for others rather than separating ourselves from them, when we love our enemies rather than demonizing them, when we care for the imprisoned rather than building higher walls.

For a couple years, when I was growing up, my family lived in a small rural town in Eastern Oregon. Public school there was really bad so they enrolled my brother and I in a private school: a conservative Christian school. Even now I can look back and see that it was a fine place to learn, and it didn't harm me to learn even the more conservative Christian elements that I might find unacceptable now. This school was a place with zero tolerance for things that were forbidden. Dancing, candy, make-up, gum, public displays of affection (like holding hands), immodest dress and inappropriate language were all strictly forbidden. Being the new kid in an environment like that was hard. Most of the other children seemed very devoted to such rules, and clearly had no experience other than obedience. On one occasion, while out at recess, I nearly faced a reprimand for using a word my classmates had never heard and therefore didn't know the meaning of, so they assumed it must obviously be on the forbidden list. I don't recall the exact context, but while talking with a small group on the playground I used the unknown word and was immediately reported to our teacher. No friendship or bond among school mates was stronger than the requirement to report rule breaking of ANY kind. In other words, tattling was the norm in all circumstances. The teacher was informed I had used a "bad word," she came over to regard our group, she made the student whisper the word in her ear and, with deeply furrowed brow and a very stern unhappy look, addressed me directly while all the students in earshot stood witness. She said, "The word 'prejudice' is not a bad word, but it is to be used with care and caution!" I was not technically punished or scolded, but clearly I was supposed to feel chastised and warned. That day, however, I felt vindication in the judgment of my teacher before the court of my classmates, but it never happened again.

Imagine my relief when, halfway through the year, a new girl joined our class having just moved to town with her family. I was relieved not to be 'the new kid' anymore, but thought it would be short-lived. I had moved to this small community from a larger city, but Denise was clearly a country kid and I thought she would get along better. Denise was strong, had calloused hands and clearly had chores at home, so I thought she would fit in soon enough and my status as the new kid would return. But she was also "new to the faith" so to speak, and had a hard time remembering all the rules. She wore jeans regularly, which, while technically not against the rules, was frowned upon. She would regularly have something sweet in her lunch, which was usually reported and confiscated even though it was packed by her mother, and she occasionally would wear just the slightest bit of make-up, which, if noticed, she had to scrub off at the sink in our classroom rather than being sent to the restroom. Denise had a very hard time fitting in.

One morning, shortly after class had begun, one of the girls seated near Denise shot her hand up in the air and, when called on, declared that Denise was "hiding a big piece of candy in her desk." Each student in our class sat at an old-style desk, the kind where the top lifted up revealing storage inside for books, papers and school supplies. In response to the accusation, our teacher came to Denise's desk and questioned her. She denied having any candy. The girl who had tattled in the first place spoke up and said she was lying, then a couple other girls nearby spoke up and also claimed to have seen a "big wad of candy." Denise still denied it. This went back and forth for a few moments, then the teacher insisted on searching her desk. Her initial inspection found nothing, but when she rummaged deeper she discovered a tiny piece of chewed gum hidden under writing supplies. When it was held up for inspection, the tattling girls said "SEE!" and I was stunned. The "big wad of candy" was a chewed piece of gum not even the size of a pencil eraser, yet Denise was led out of the class and taken to the principal's office to be punished.

Denise could have claimed the gum had always been in the desk. In any other school, gum stuck to a desk would be understood, maybe even expected, but not here. She could have claimed she was chewing the gum on the way to school and just forgot, which is so obviously what had happened, yet rules were more important than grace in that place. The amazing thing that I have discovered since this childhood experience is that many of our churches, and especially denominations, are exactly like this.

In Matthew 25, where Jesus tells the parable that is the theme for this book, the church leaders of his day are in the process of plotting to get rid of Jesus. And in every generation there have been movements among the people of faith to do the exact same thing. There are always leaders who insist on focusing on rules rather than relationship, defending personal power rather than the divine direction to love, and creating doctrine and dogma that serve an organization and "good order" rather than serving the neighbor. These selfish desires have, in every generation, sought to lead backward rather than forward. Defense of order and organization holds on to the past, does not allow creative engagement with the present, and allows no room for change and growth into the future. While we constantly attempt to deny the reality of decline that has been happening in the church (all churches) for a generation, we can put our heads in the sand no longer.

Denise and I were imprisoned back in our school days. Lots of kids claim school is like prison, and of course it is childish melodrama, but in my adult reflection on this childhood experience I am convinced it was exactly that. And it is probably true that the culture of the children was created by the culture of the adults in charge of the school, and maybe the larger culture of a denomination, but it was certainly human construction regardless. This isn't a statement about education, or private vs. public schools, or discipline, or anything like those.

It is an example of how people of faith, and organizations, are far more comfortable constructing prisons than we are at living with freedom. And we are called, as people of faith, as followers of Jesus, to comfort the imprisoned, not tighten their shackles. We are called to bring light into the dark dungeons where people are, not double bolt the door. We are called to speak out against oppression, not build better jails.

It is an irony that in a time when churches are struggling in every way, when attendance is dwindling, finances are challenging, and our relevance is constantly being questioned, that our enforcing of dogmatic rules and boundaries would turn out to be our largest focus. It makes sense though; during times of change and uncertainty it is human nature to want to hold on to something familiar. Holding to the rules, laws and boundaries of a previous generation is the path of least resistance, and does not require discernment or study. But don't make the additional lazy argument that this is suggesting we just throw out the rules, history and tradition. There is a large amount of real estate between blindly following the rules of the past and tossing them all out. It requires work, discernment and change that most people, and organizations, are not willing to do.

The way forward for the church is not reinforcing the past, nor recreating that which has been lost. For whether we want to admit it or not, the church of the past is lost. Our culture has chosen to vacate the cathedral that seeks to control them. Will we simply wave goodbye to the people who have left our church, hold to the belief that we are right and they must be wrong and therefore doomed? Or will we honestly question our purpose, and practice, as a community? Will we change? Which of those options seems more faithful to the leader who commends his followers saying "I was in prison and you visited me"?

In the summer of 2010 my family and I spent time at a retreat center called Holden Village. Holden Village is a remote retreat center located in the Cascade Mountains of Washington State. While at this place I spent time with a friend and colleague named Mark Pedersen. At that time Mark and I were serving congregations in neighboring towns in Oregon. I shared with Mark the way I was being inspired by the image of cairns, and the connection I was finding to Matthew 25. We talked and shared and pondered, then we were stirred to action. I don't recall which of us turned to the other and said, "Let's build a cairn!" but it was mutual.

Holden Village was originally a large copper mine, and across the river from the village are the remains of the mine. There was a vast expanse of tailings left from the years of mining operation, and between the tailings and the old mine was a large hillside of scree - loose rock and debris also left over from the mining operations. On a flat patch near the bottom of that scree field, beside a trail, is where we decided to start.

One example of a cairn (a purposeful pile of rocks) is the bee-hive hermitages that can be found in some remote parts of the world. In some places there are whole villages of huts made by piling rocks in a circle that gets smaller as it gets higher, until it is enclosed at the top. This is the type of cairn Mark and I set out to create, although on a smaller scale.

At the bottom of the hill of scree, in an area covered with loose rock, wood and debris, we found a circle of smooth flat dirt about eight feet across. Right in the middle of the circle was a tidy pile of deer droppings. We decided to leave the pile undisturbed, and build around it. As we gathered rocks and built our circular pile, we talked and considered what this would mean to those who came after us. What trail were we marking? I don't recall a good answer to that; we were just being creative and having fun.

Soon after we started, we found the remains of a metal chair. Just trash at first glance, but something about it stirred us. The seat was rusted and the whole chair had been crushed. The legs were bent and folded under as if the chair were on its knees, and the back was flattened as if it were looking up to heaven. For whatever reason it captured our attention and we stared for several moments. Then Mark said, "It looks like something from Guantanamo Bay." It was a powerful image and did in fact convey tortured submission. Controversy over the prison in Cuba had been in the news frequently, and had been on our minds. We placed the chair in the center of our cairn, directly above the tidy pile of droppings, and continued building. We left no openings, just the gaps between rocks, and in the end our cairn was about five feet tall, and it was the monument we had envisioned.

As we pondered what our monument might mean, or what we were marking, we wrote a poem, etched it on a board and mounted it next to our cairn.

We Watch The Trail Go By,
And The Tailings Nye,
With Mountain, God & You.
At Our Heart Is A Place Of Suffering
& Also A Place To Sit.
After The Fall, At The End Of All,
We Are Just Rock, And Dirt, And ...

Mark and I continued to talk from time to time about cairns as a spiritual image and metaphor, and some months later he and I spent time on a beach, me piling rocks and Mark taking creative pictures of them. Those became the artwork for this book. But we have never forgotten the cairn we built near Holden village that summer. There is a picture of our efforts on the last page of this book.

I assume that someone, sometime, took notice of our pile of rocks, and maybe our poem, but would it mean anything to them? It doesn't matter. It was a labor of creative expression that was cathartic in its own way, and for its own sake. But it occurs to me that the pile of rocks Mark and I made with meaning and conviction means nothing to those who weren't with us, and that is how the church looks to those outside it.

For Further Reflection or Discussion

- What are some of the things keeping people imprisoned in society today?

- Is there guilt or regret that you have held onto? If so, how long?

- How has the church imprisoned people in the past? How is it now?

- Do you believe your denomination is better than others? Why? What does being 'right' get you?

- How might you live your life of faith in such a way that it frees others from the burdens they carry?

Scripture for further consideration
Read Acts 16:25-34

Paul and Silas in prison still understand that they are servants of God. Singing, worshiping and proclaiming the goodness of God in all the places they find themselves. And because of their honest faithfulness, others come to know the goodness of God too.

Prayer

Dear God, we know you desire freedom for us, yet we need your help to free us from the bondage of our own making. Help us find release. And in the joy we find in freedom, may we work to set others free. In Jesus' Name, AMEN.

CHAPTER 8

Summary

"The king will answer them,
'Truly I tell you, just as you did it to one of the least
of these who are members of my family,
you did it to me."

Matt.25:40

The Way Forward

While writing this book I would occasionally reflect on the title, The Way Forward, and what it means for myself and my ministry. When I started, these three words were not as popular as they are currently. So much for being unique and original. When I started this project a simple internet search of the words "The Way Forward" led to links for marketing, sales pitches and news from a large banking corporation, the 2006 strategy for Ford Motor Company, the U.S. government's strategy for drawing down troops in Afghanistan, statements on both nuclear energy and biofuels, and many links to a company that makes video games. Now almost all of the links are to political documents, statements, or books written by politicians. It has become a hip and popular turn of phrase. That being said, I hope this is not seen as a new marketing strategy for your church, or the latest program slogan. I hope you are simply reminded that this has been our path all along, and even though God is leading us to a place we can't yet see or understand, nothing but good comes from our caring for others and following faithfully the trail that is set before us.

I don't believe this is a book that will help save the Church. This is not about 'how we save an institution;' it is about how we continue our journey of faith in light of our changing culture, reality and world. Your church may still not be able to pay a pastor, or you may lose the building that houses your church, but the church has always been believers gathered together. What matters is what you do when you are gathered and what you do after the gathering, not where you gather, or if you can afford to pay clergy to lead you, or if you have young families in your gathering, or any of the other things that we falsely assume are the marks of "a healthy church."

In all the ways that our world is polarizing over issues of gender, race and religion, this is actually a path that can draw us together across the lines that divide us. While I have been describing "cairns" that have been trail markers for Christians for two thousand years, there are very similar tenets in the Jewish tradition, the Muslim faith, and the basic teaching of every major religion.

If a community of people is committed to care for those in need, any concern about 'who will care for me' goes away, because there is always someone behind us on the trail, following the 'cairns' we have followed and built stronger with our own faithfulness and service.

We live in a time of great uncertainty, and it seems to be getting greater all the time. The anxiety that we are feeling as a society because of this uncertainty continues to tempt us in two directions: back to what we falsely believe were better times, or inward, hunkering down and building up defenses against phantoms and trumped up dangers. Our world has dangers, there is no denying that, but the world has always been dangerous, and God has always had something to say about it: *"Be still and know that I am God."* (Psalm 46:10)

"Car & Driver"

When I was young, like many church kids, I went to church camp. I don't remember the first time I played a game called "Car & Driver" because I have played it so many times since whenever that was. It has also come to illustrate a deep spiritual understanding for me that has helped guide me on my journey.

The game works like this. Take your group to a wide open space, like a ball field or meadow. Divide the group into pairs, and each pair gets one blindfold. One person is designated as the "car" and wears the blindfold, while the other person is the "driver." "Driving" instructions are very simple. You don't drive a car by talking to it, so this game is played silently. To accelerate, the "driver" lightly taps the "car" on the back. To steer, the "driver" lightly taps the "car" on each arm in the direction they wish to go. To brake, the "driver" gently lays their hands on both shoulders until the car has come to a stop. When the leader says, each pair switches roles.

Regardless of the age of the participants there will inevitably be some drivers who take their car "off-road," there may be a crash or two, and hopefully each participant has a moment or two of doubt. A moment when they are the "car" being driven, and because they are going the direction the driver desires, they don't feel the driver behind them. They begin to doubt the driver - their ability to drive, their concern for the "car's" welfare, or even their presence. Maybe the "driver" is playing a trick and driving off a cliff! When the leader processes the experience with the group it is a great opportunity for conversations about giving and receiving trust, about care for others, and about who, or what, "drives" us.

The spiritual implications here can run very deep. In a journey of faith we pray for God to be the one who guides us, who "drives" us, as we try to follow God's directions. But how often do we feel God's presence? Some people feel it all the time, but many of us have only occasional experiences of God's direction, along with periods of silence in between. Many great people of faith have talked about "the silence of God." God is not absent during those times, although it may feel like it. It is during these times that we need to be patient and faithful in continuing in the same direction, trusting that when we need to turn, stop, or go faster, God will "steer" us.

In my own life there have been many times when I can say with certainty that God was directing my path, and there are far more times when I had the trust that God was there but I couldn't prove it or feel it. It's during those times that I have just tried to continue the course I am on, serving faithfully, until guidance comes to change direction.

Isn't that where we are as the church? There are so many things that we have done, created, been a part of, and been distracted by that have led us to where we are today. Blame is not useful. Finding the way forward is hard. And in many ways we are like the Hebrews of the Old Testament: nomads. It may seem as if we are wandering, but if we seek the cairns that mark the trail of faith we will eventually get to where we are going. For now it may feel trite to say, but our life of faith is about the journey, not the destination. So let us keep our feet on the path.

Jews are sometimes referred to as 'People of the Book.' "The Book," the Torah, is the story of God and God's people. A teaching in Judaism is that Jews do not have doctrine, they have story. And the story they know from the Torah is ongoing and forever unfolding.

Christians are often called 'People of the Way.' Jesus said "I am the way, and the truth, and the life." (John 14:6) Early

Christians were referred to as those who followed "the Way." But in today's practice, in so many instances, the church has become "people of the way-side", or "people of the rest stop." The motion of the followers of Jesus has slowed considerably, and we have been content to plant ourselves rather than travel the path our Lord is leading us on. For a while it might have seemed good and wise to build buildings, brand them as denominational, and try to fill them with similar people, but that took us away from the path.

In finding our way forward through this emerging time we need to reconnect with "The Way." The Way is not a place, or a list for doing things right, it is a person: Jesus. This Jesus leads us on a journey, and, to be honest, it is a bit of a hike.

I found this quotation from William Faulkner and I think it speaks to the cairns that are our trail markers for our journey of faith. Every purposeful pile of rocks, piled for a reason, has the potential to become a monument (or cathedral). As such, it is in our nature to venerate monuments. This stalls our journey and even draws us away from the path that leads us forward. So rather than monuments, maybe we should see even our most ornate monuments as footprints. Speaking of a symphony Faulkner says this,

> *"They are not monuments, but footprints. A monument only says 'At least I got this far,' while a footprint says 'This is where I was when I moved again.'"*

[William Faulkner, quoted in Sam di Bonaventura's Program Notes to Elie Siegmeister's Symphony No. 5, Baltimore Symphony Concert, May 5, 1977]

[from A Long Obedience in the Same Direction by Eugene H. Peterson, p. 17. Inter Varsity Press, 1980.]

The Church in this Emergent Time

I know this is a fearful time. The unknown looms large in front of us. What will survive the changes we are undergoing as a society? What will the church look like in 10, 20 or 50 years? Who will care for the church when we are gone? Will there still be someone to bury me when I die? These, and many more, are not trivial questions. There is fear and anxiety all around us. Rather than fight, or defend, or shore up, or build walls, it is time to lace up our hiking shoes and take the steps of faith that have always led us forward as we follow Jesus.

Here is another difficult reality about this time. In many faith communities, of every denomination, there are those who have means, and are insistent that things go back to the way they were. It is difficult to have this conversation in affluent congregations. The change in our society and world is obvious and unstoppable, yet we want things to go back to the way they were. The realities of church decline are undeniable, yet we want to deny them. What the church will look like in the future is uncertain, yet we insist that strategic planning is needed before we can move forward. But whether we want to or not, we are going forward. We can not un-change society. We can not stop church decline by doing the same old things. And we won't find our way forward with a better capital campaign.

In many churches the decline is threatening the very existence of the congregation. Deferred maintenance and increased costs to maintain the building, shrinking attendance, little or no resources to pay staff or clergy, and the real possibility of the church "going out of business" all create a desperate openness to conversation. In such a place a congregation is open to discuss changing everything, and open to re-think what it means to be the church. But they have come to that place by force, and have lost the capacity to think creatively and have the conversation constructively. Whereas larger congregations, places with resources and capacity, tend to convince themselves that they don't need to have that conversation. Convinced that they have been more successful than those other churches, they resolve to continue as they have for so long. Small seasons of decline are simply to be weathered by budget cuts and tightening the belt. They conclude that because they still have a pastoral staff and Sunday School program that works, things will come back around eventually. Very few of the congregations that have resources and capacity are even entertaining the conversation about changing how church is done.

If congregations that have capacity and resources would see themselves as leaders in re-inventing the church, there could be real change in the future of the small struggling congregations. If they could see themselves as laboratories rather than ivory towers, that might be a start. And the conversation needs to include questions, hard questions. Can you imagine your congregation having an identity without a building or paid staff? We say things like "the church is not a building," but do we really mean it? And clergy have to be brave enough to lead the conversation. As church professionals we are reluctant to have conversations that might challenge our livelihood. But doesn't the church closing do that too? We need to remind ourselves that God is faithful. When we believe it, and live according to it, our congregations will do likewise.

The Church in this Emergent Time

For a very long time we have been devoting ourselves to the piling up of rocks as monuments. We have built churches with deep meaning and symbolism, large impressive structures with grand instruments, and we have offered extensive interpretation. But the meaning is still being lost over time. We have built monuments rather than markers.

The way forward is not found in programs or personnel, but in the person who has always been "The Way." Following Jesus has always been our way forward. Jesus has always been "the way, and the truth, and the life" even when we fight over stuff, disagree, and wander off the path. This book won't fix a broken world, won't heal a hurting church, and won't save a dying age. But I am convinced that we can find our way through all of our struggles if we keep our feet on the path that has been ours since the beginning. It is no simple thing to follow this path: feed the hungry, quench the thirsty, welcome the stranger, clothe the naked, care for the sick, minister to the imprisoned. And on this path we are never left alone.

"Remember, I am with you always, to the end of the age." (Matt. 28:20b)

Not long ago my wife and I became "empty-nesters." Our children have gone to college, and are independent. Although there is no way of knowing with absolute certainty, it appears as if they have left home and are off to begin lives of their own. There will be extended visits to be sure, but for the most part they are off into the world. The day my daughter left I had the following reflection.

<u>Standing on the very edge ...</u>
Standing in my back yard, looking out at the landscape, barely noticing all the things that need trimming or attention, something is altogether different.

Different even from this morning.

This morning I took my daughter to the airport so she could go to Oregon and work all summer as a lifeguard at a summer camp. A month ago she graduated from high school and at the end of the summer she will start college. She is our youngest, which means as I stand in the yard this evening, I am standing on the very edge of what was and what comes next. Like standing on an actual line that, once crossed can't be uncrossed, I know that there is no going back. I can only go forward.

It is an emotional thing. Fear and pride and anxiety and excitement all mingle together. A small part of me does wish that things could stay the same, but a very small part. I know in my heart, not just my head, that this has to be and that this change is good and right. Still emotions swirl.

We have been preparing for this day, all of us, making the most of every little thing, especially over the last month. We have always done that. We have tried purposefully to get the most out of every stage of our lives, and especially our lives together, so that there are very few longings we have for places or times where we have been. So, I don't want to go back. I don't want to hold on to this moment. And at the same time I can not ignore the powerful significance of the line on which I stand. So I pause and take it in, allowing the moment to be profound.

It is more than a metaphor, it is an actual thing. As I pause in this moment, taking stock, wondering, acknowledging the significance, I know I can not take even one step back. I can only step forward, . . . but I can wait just a moment. What comes next I don't know. A reality people tell us about, but what does it mean to be "empty-nesters"? Jokes about mid-life crises and red sports cars, but what will it really be? The only way is forward, and we figure it out as we go.

My daughter and I went for a long, hot run this morning, we washed off and cooled down, then we ate together, packed and loaded up for a late morning flight. We had all talked of how we wanted the morning to go, and that helped us get what we each needed in saying goodbye. It went as planned. Emotion but not stress. Sad but happy. And now at home, I stand in the back yard looking at nothing, seeing the reality, standing on the very edge of what has been and what is about to be.

Long pause, deep breath, with a tear on my cheek . . . I step.

For Further Reflection or Discussion

- What are your fears about the future of the church?

- Have there been times in your life when you didn't feel God's direction? How did you handle it?

- What is the most difficult part of the author's question "Can you imagine your congregation having an identity without a building or paid staff"?

- What change do you have the most difficulty with in your life?

- Where do we go from here?

Scripture for further consideration
Read Matthew 28:16-20 and Romans 8:38-39

This passage from Matthew is often called "The Great Commission" and it is Jesus' last words to the disciples in the Gospel of Matthew. Two things to take note of: even at this point in the story some of the disciples doubted, and Jesus still promises to be with them always. The passage from Paul's letter to the early church in Rome is a common funeral text. Paul lists all the things that WILL NOT separate us from the Love of God. I would add the following to his list: failure, rituals, sacraments, monuments and denominations.

Prayer

O God, you have called your servants to ventures of which we cannot see the ending, by paths as yet untrodden, through perils unknown. Give us faith to go out with good courage, not knowing where we go, but only that your hand is leading us and your love supporting us; through Jesus Christ our Lord. AMEN.

Thank You

A special thank you to Barbara Rintala,
whose encouragement was constant
and whose editorial work made this book far less
offensive due to garmantical error.

Rev. Mark Pedersen, illustrator (left) and
Rev. Jeff Kallevig, author (right)
beside a cairn they build together in Railroad Valley
near Holden Village, WA in the summer of 2010

Thank You

Thank you Mark, for your friendship,
your encouragement, your creativity and your photography.
Let's meet at Holden Village again soon.